P9-APK-700

student study
ART NOTEBOOK

FIFTH EDITION

BIOLOGY

Sylvia S. Mader

WCB **Wm. C. Brown Publishers**

Dubuque, IA Bogota Boston Buenos Aires Caracas Chicago
Guilford, CT London Madrid Mexico City Sydney Toronto

 **A Times Mirror Company**

COVER CREDIT: © Manfred Danegger/Peter Arnold, Inc.

The credits section for this book begins on page 000 and
is considered an extension of the copyright page.

Copyright © 1996 Times Mirror Higher Education Group, Inc.
All rights reserved

LISBN 0–697–28182–5

No part of this publication may be reproduced, stored in a retrieval
system, or transmitted, in any form or by any means, electronic,
mechanical, photocopying, recording, or otherwise, without the
prior written permission of the publisher.

Printed in the United States of America by Times Mirror Higher Education Group, Inc.,
2460 Kerper Boulevard, Dubuque, IA 52001

10 9 8 7 6 5 4 3 2 1

TO INSTRUCTORS AND STUDENTS

This Student Study Art Notebook is a tool to assist students in note taking during lectures. On each page, there are one, two, three, or sometimes four figures faithfully reproduced from the textbook. Each figure also corresponds to one of the 300 acetates available to instructors who adopt the textbook.

The intention is to place the acetate art in front of students (via the notebook) as the instructor uses the overhead during lectures. The advantage to the student is that he/she will be able to see all labels clearly, and take meaningful notes without having to make hurried sketches of the acetate figure.

The pages of the Art Notebook are perforated and three-hole punched, so they can be removed and placed in a personal binder for specific study and review, or to create space for additional notes.

DIRECTORY OF NOTEBOOK FIGURES

TO ACCOMPANY
SYLVIA S. MADER *BIOLOGY, 5/e*

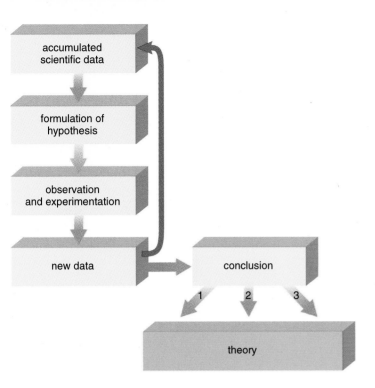

Scientific Method
Figure 2.1

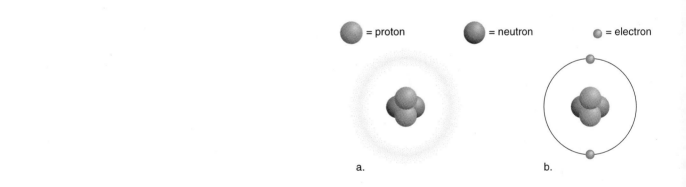

Helium Atom
Figure 3.2

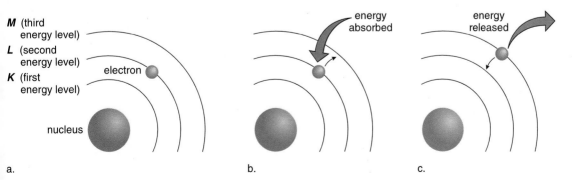

Electron Energy Levels
Figure 3.4

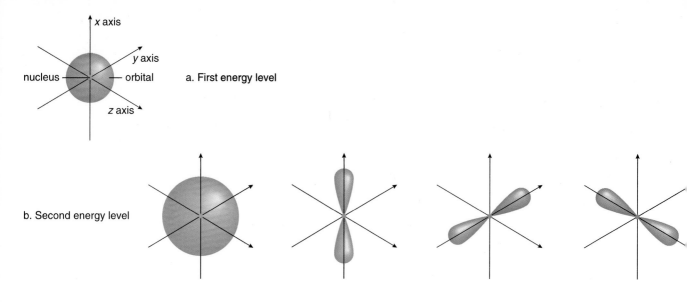

a. First energy level

x axis
y axis
z axis
nucleus — orbital

b. Second energy level

Electron Orbitals
Figure 3.5

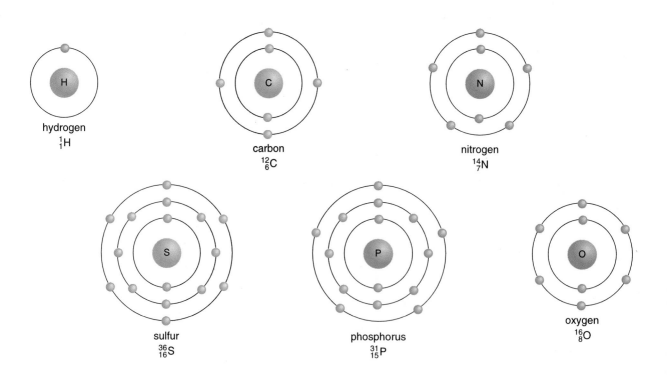

hydrogen
^1_1H

carbon
$^{12}_6C$

nitrogen
$^{14}_7N$

sulfur
$^{36}_{16}S$

phosphorus
$^{31}_{15}P$

oxygen
$^{16}_8O$

Bohr Models of Atoms
Figure 3.6

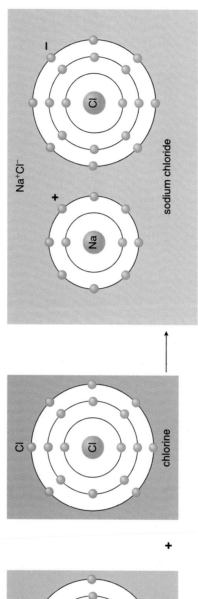

Ionic Reaction
Figure 3.7a

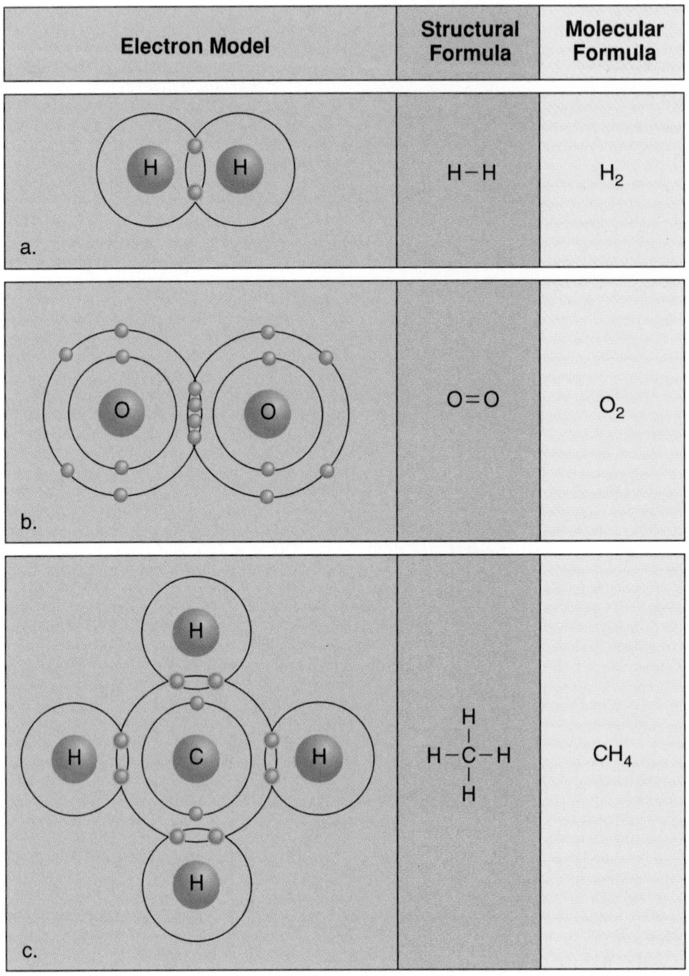

Electron Model	Structural Formula	Molecular Formula
a.	H–H	H_2
b.	O=O	O_2
c.	H–C–H with H above and H below	CH_4

Covalent Bonding
Figure 3.9

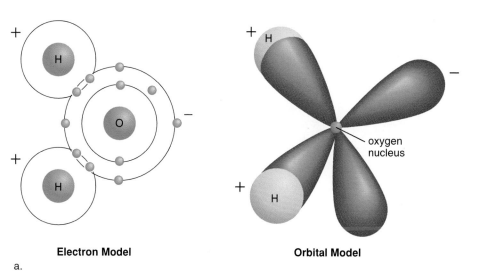

Electron Model

Orbital Model

oxygen nucleus

Space-Filling Model

a.

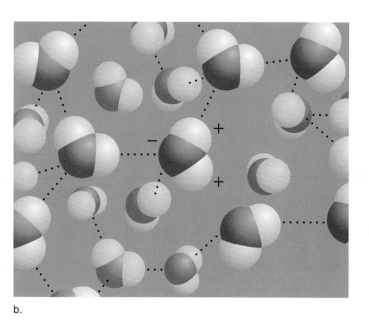

b.

Water Molecule
Figure 3.10

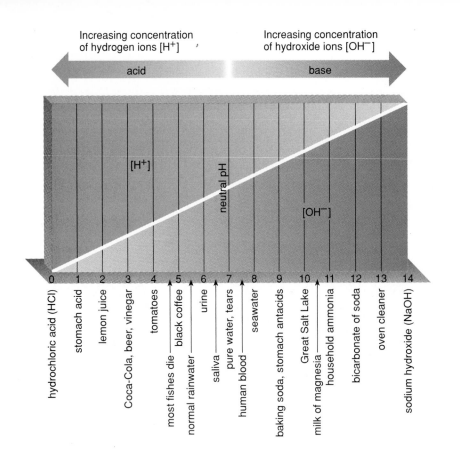

pH Scale
Figure 3.14

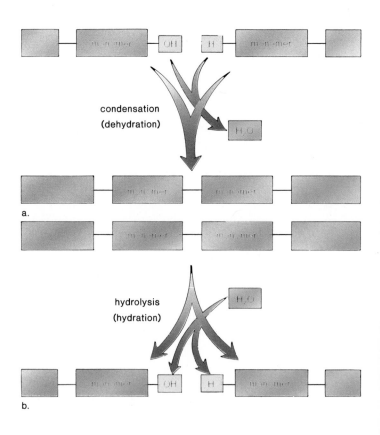

Synthesis and Breakdown of Polymers
Figure 4.4

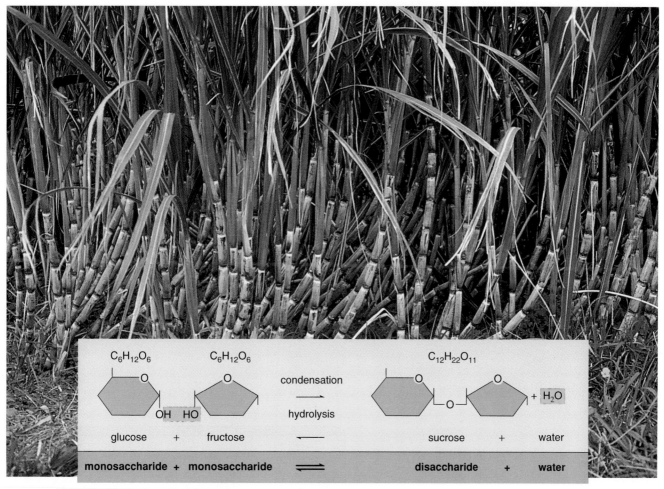

b.

Disaccharide Formation and Breakdown
Figure 4.6

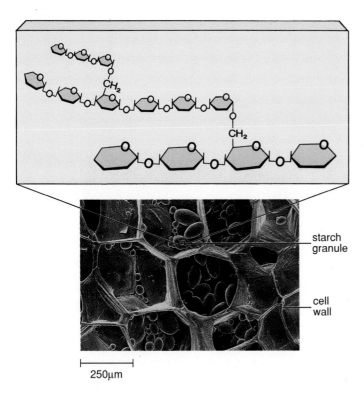

a. Starch Structure
Figure 4.7

250μm

starch
granule

cell
wall

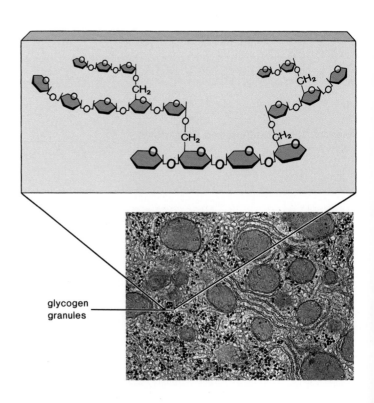

glycogen
granules

b. Glycogen Structure
Figure 4.7*b*

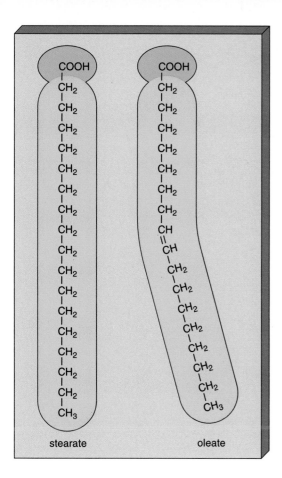

Fatty Acid Structure
Figure 4.9

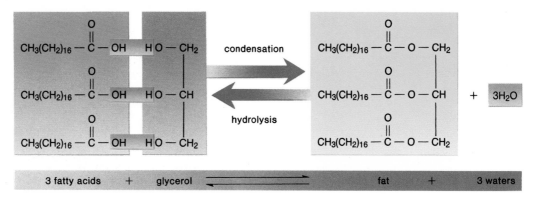

Formation of a Neutral Fat
Figure 4.10

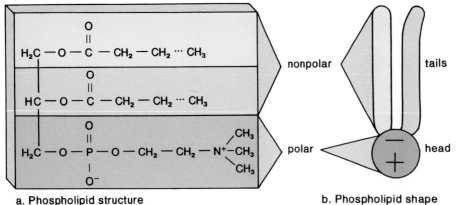

nonpolar
polar
tails
head
a. Phospholipid structure
b. Phospholipid shape

Phospholipid Structure
Figure 4.12

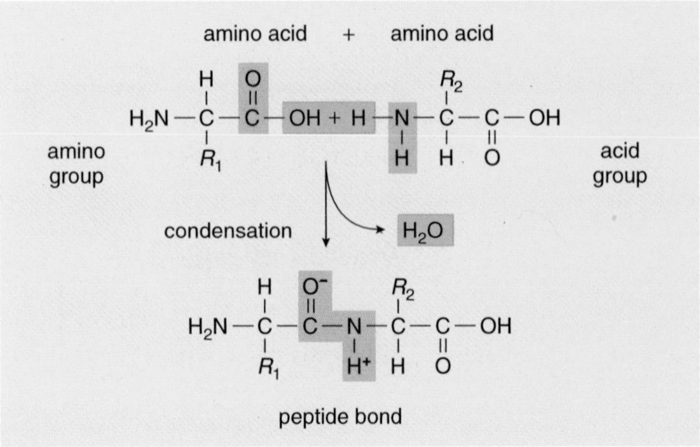

amino acid + amino acid
amino group
acid group
condensation
H2O
peptide bond

Synthesis of a Peptide
Figure 4.14

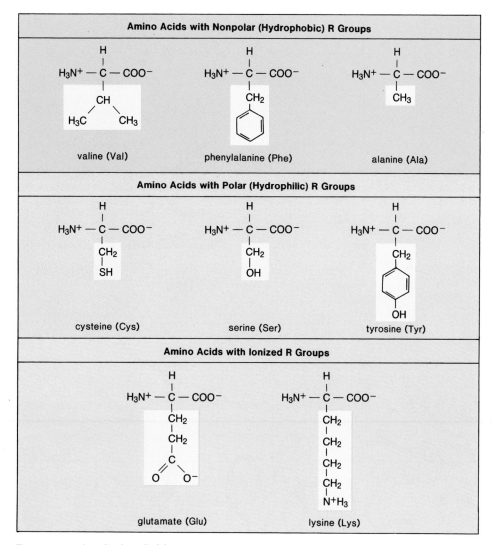

Representative Amino Acids
Figure 4.15

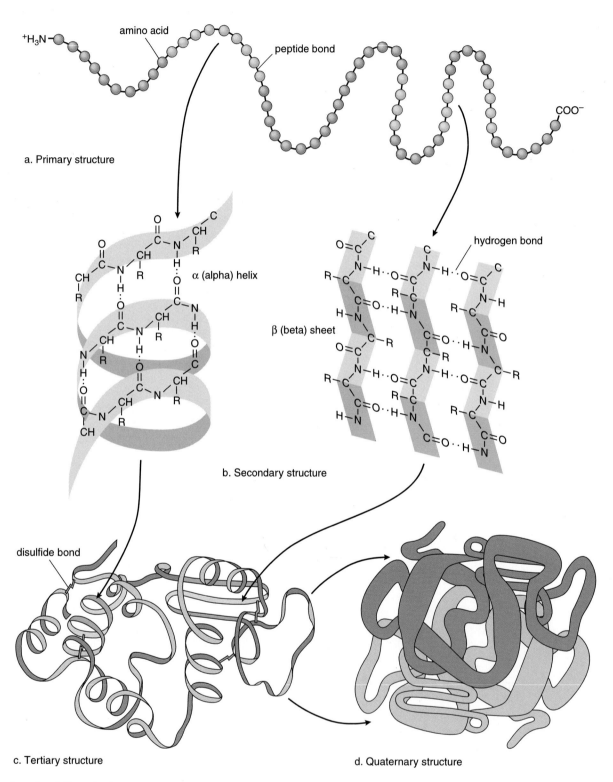

a. Primary structure

amino acid

peptide bond

^+H_3N—

COO$^-$

α (alpha) helix

β (beta) sheet

hydrogen bond

b. Secondary structure

disulfide bond

c. Tertiary structure

d. Quaternary structure

Levels of Protein Structure
Figure 4.18

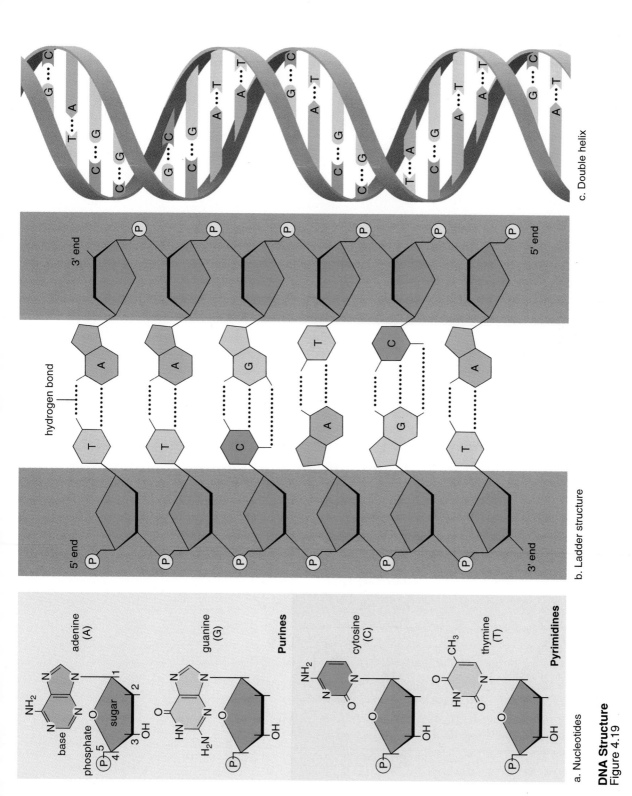

DNA Structure
Figure 4.19

a. Nucleotides

adenine (A)

guanine (G)

Purines

cytosine (C)

thymine (T)

Pyrimidines

base

phosphate

sugar

b. Ladder structure

hydrogen bond

5' end

3' end

3' end

5' end

c. Double helix

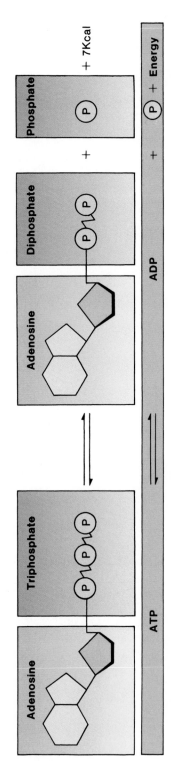

ATP Reaction
Figure 4.20

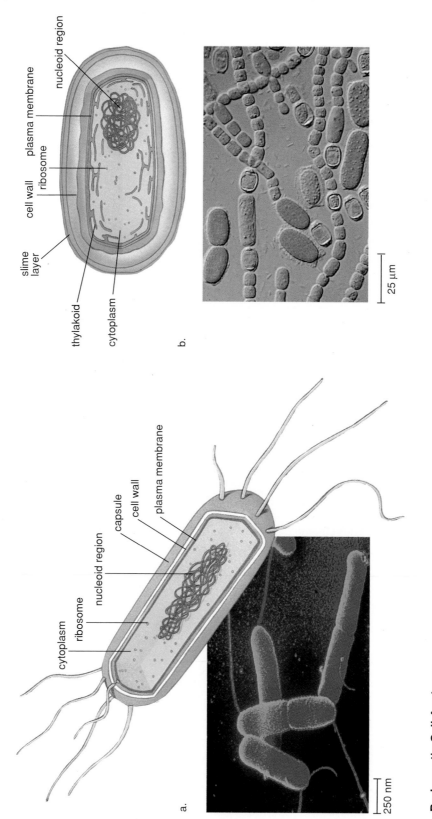

nucleoid region

plasma membrane

cell wall
ribosome

slime
layer

thylakoid

cytoplasm

b.

25 μm

capsule
cell wall
plasma membrane

nucleoid region

cytoplasm
ribosome

a.

250 nm

Prokaryotic Cell Anatomy
Figure 5.3

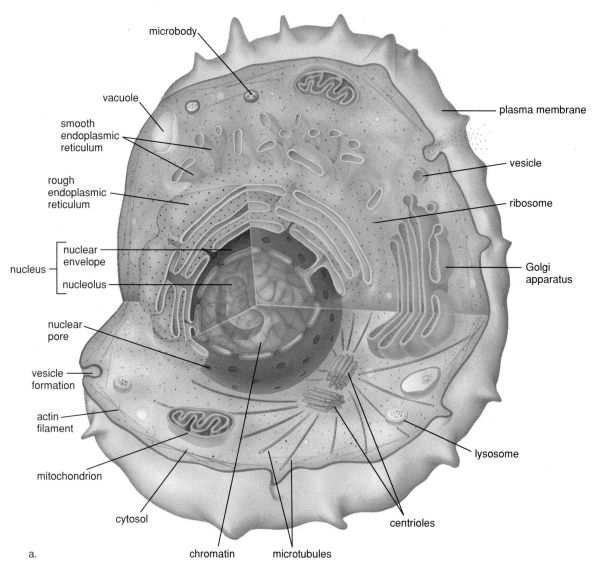

microbody

vacuole

smooth
endoplasmic
reticulum

rough
endoplasmic
reticulum

nucleus

nuclear
envelope

nucleolus

nuclear
pore

vesicle
formation

actin
filament

mitochondrion

cytosol

plasma membrane

vesicle

ribosome

Golgi
apparatus

lysosome

centrioles

chromatin

microtubules

a.

Animal Cell Anatomy
Figure 5.4*a*

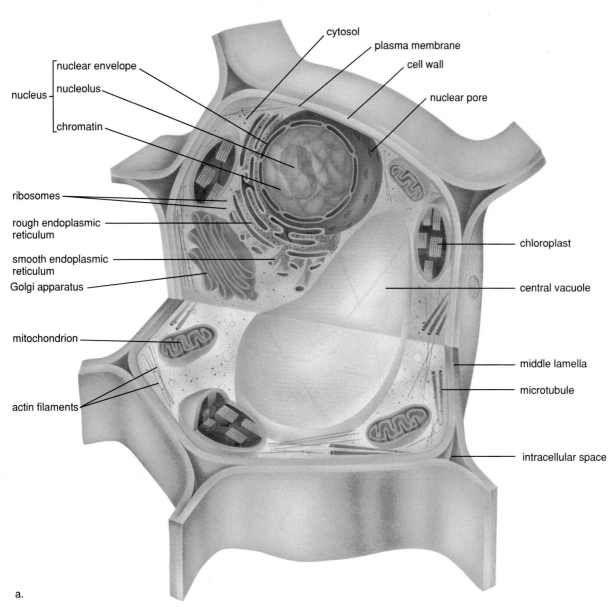

cytosol

plasma membrane

cell wall

nuclear envelope

nuclear pore

nucleus

nucleolus

chromatin

ribosomes

rough endoplasmic reticulum

chloroplast

smooth endoplasmic reticulum

Golgi apparatus

central vacuole

mitochondrion

middle lamella

microtubule

actin filaments

intracellular space

a.

Plant Cell Anatomy
Figure 5.5a

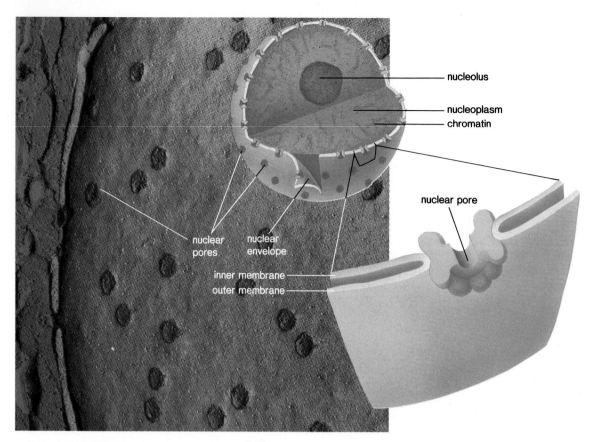

nucleolus

nucleoplasm

chromatin

nuclear pore

nuclear pores

nuclear envelope

inner membrane

outer membrane

Anatomy of the Nucleus
Figure 5.6

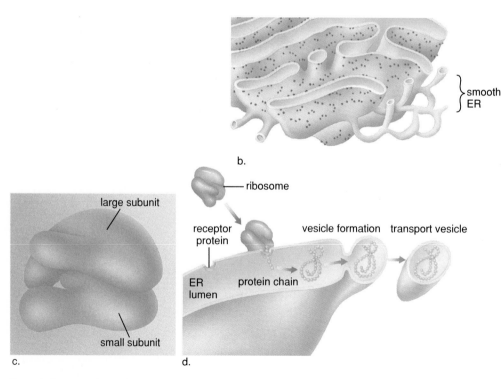

smooth ER

b.

ribosome

large subunit

receptor protein

vesicle formation   transport vesicle

ER lumen

protein chain

small subunit

c.

d.

Rough Endoplasmic Reticulum
Figure 5.7*b,c,d*

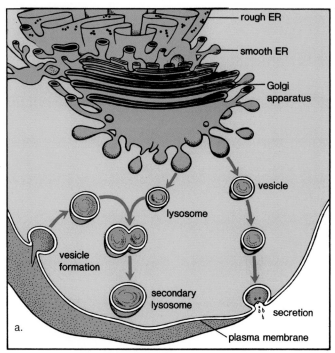

Function of Golgi Apparatus

Golgi Apparatus
Figure 5.8*b*

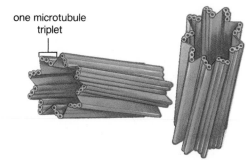

a. Centrioles

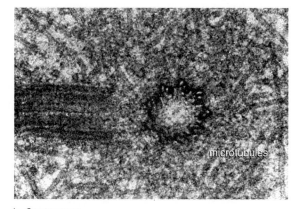

b. Centrosome

Centrioles
Figure 5.14

19

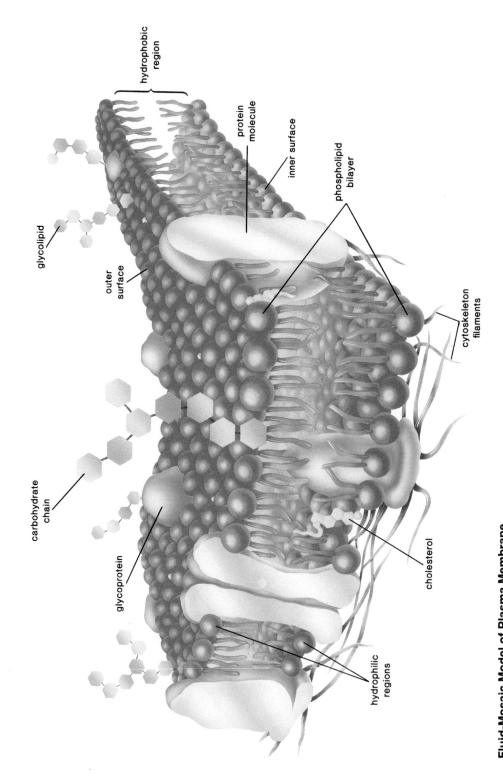

hydrophobic region

glycolipid

outer surface

protein molecule

inner surface

phospholipid bilayer

cytoskeleton filaments

carbohydrate chain

glycoprotein

cholesterol

hydrophilic regions

Fluid-Mosaic Model of Plasma Membrane
Figure 6.3

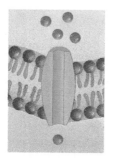

Channel Protein
Allows a particular molecule or ion to cross the plasma membrane freely. Cystic fibrosis, an inherited disorder, is caused by a faulty chloride (Cl⁻) channel; a thick mucus collects in airways and in pancreatic and liver ducts.

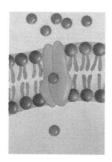

Carrier Protein
Selectively interacts with a specific molecule or ion so that it can cross the plasma membrane. The inability of some persons to use energy for sodium – potassium (Na⁺ – K⁺) transport has been suggested as the cause of their obesity.

Cell Recognition Protein
The MHC (major histocompatibility complex) glycoproteins are different for each person, so organ transplants are difficult to achieve. Cells with foreign MHC glycoproteins are attacked by blood cells responsible for immunity.

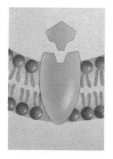

Receptor Protein
Is shaped in such a way that a specific molecule can bind to it. Pygmies are short, not because they do not produce enough growth hormone, but because their plasma membrane growth hormone receptors are faulty and cannot interact with growth hormone.

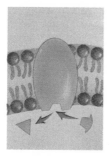

Enzymatic Protein
Catalyzes a specific reaction. The membrane protein, adenylate cyclase, is involved in ATP metabolism. Cholera bacteria release a toxin that interferes with the proper functioning of adenylate cyclase; sodium ions and water leave intestinal cells and the individual dies from severe diarrhea.

Membrane Protein Diversity
Figure 6.5

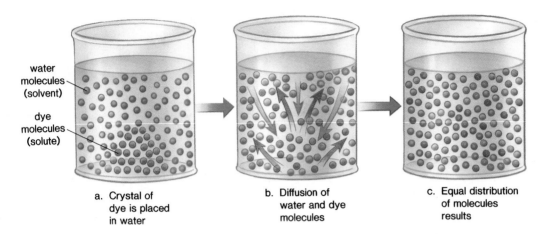

a. Crystal of dye is placed in water

b. Diffusion of water and dye molecules

c. Equal distribution of molecules results

Process of Diffusion
Figure 6.6

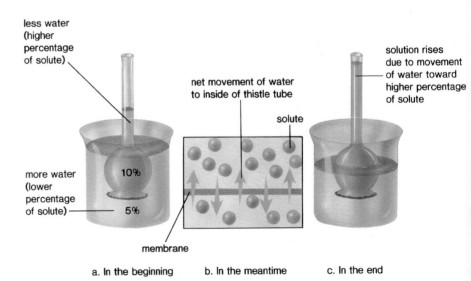

less water (higher percentage of solute)

net movement of water to inside of thistle tube

solute

more water (lower percentage of solute)

10%

5%

solution rises due to movement of water toward higher percentage of solute

membrane

a. In the beginning

b. In the meantime

c. In the end

Osmosis Demonstration
Figure 6.8

Animal Cells

a. Under isotonic conditions, there is no net movement of water.

b. In a hypotonic environment, water enters the cell, which may burst (lysis) due to osmotic pressure.

c. In a hypertonic environment, water leaves the cell, which shrivels (crenation).

Plant Cells

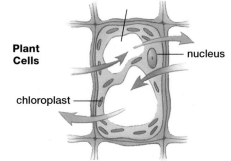
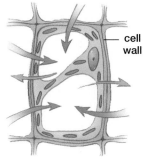
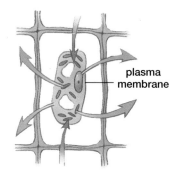

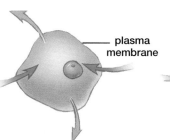

d. Under isotonic conditions, there is no net movement of water.

e. In a hypotonic environment, vacuoles fill with water, turgor pressure develops, and chloroplasts are seen next to the cell wall.

f. In a hypertonic environment, vacuoles lose water, the cytoplasm shrinks (plasmolysis), and chloroplasts are seen in the center of the cell.

Osmosis in Animal and Plant Cells
Figure 6.9

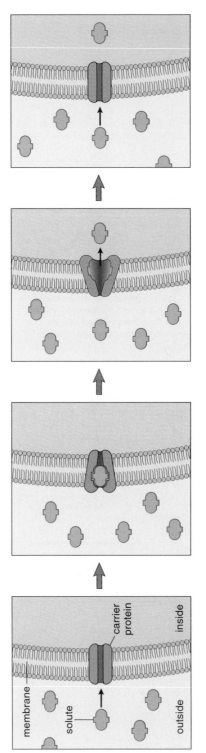

Facilitated Transport
Figure 6.10

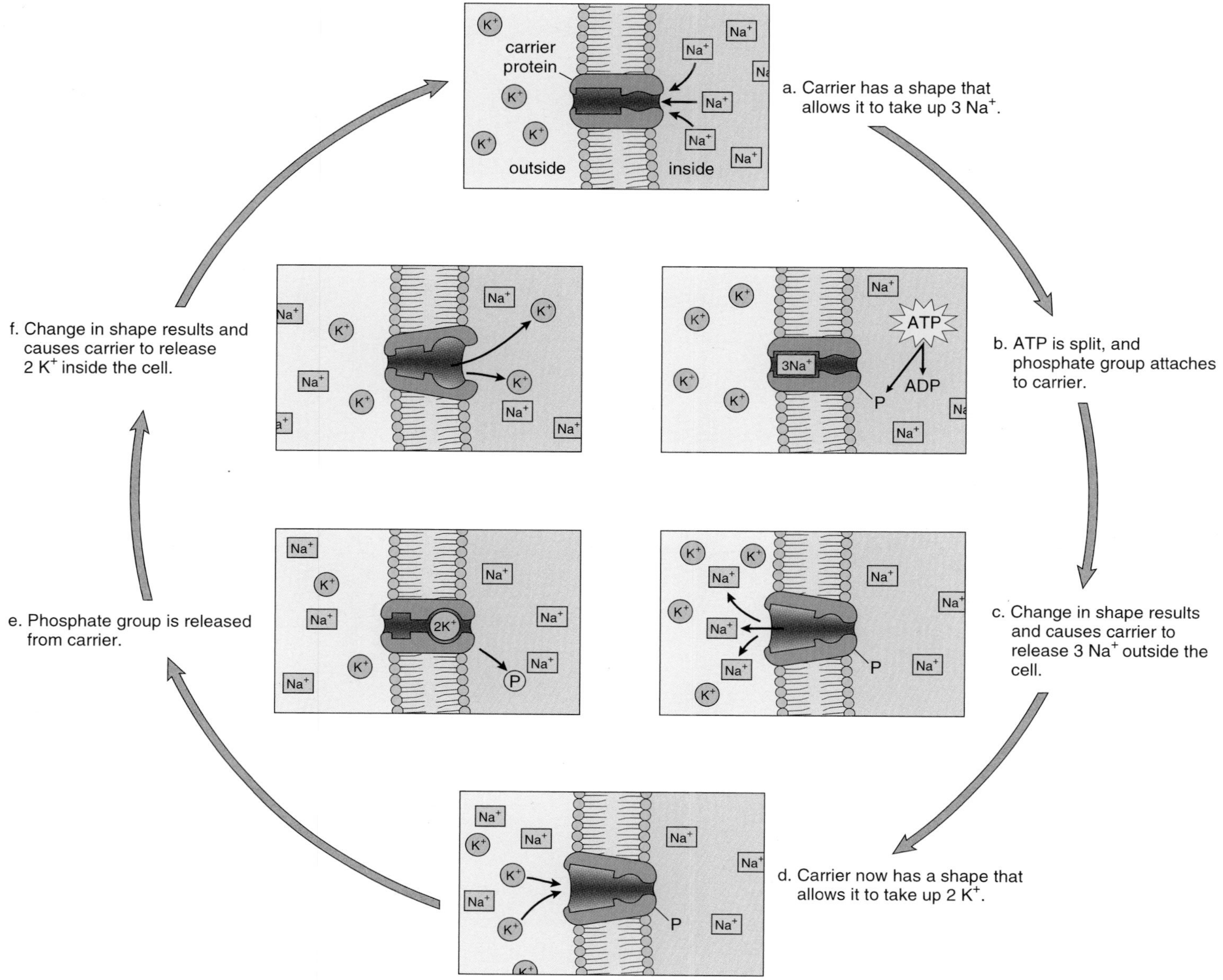

a. Carrier has a shape that allows it to take up 3 Na⁺.

b. ATP is split, and phosphate group attaches to carrier.

c. Change in shape results and causes carrier to release 3 Na⁺ outside the cell.

d. Carrier now has a shape that allows it to take up 2 K⁺.

e. Phosphate group is released from carrier.

f. Change in shape results and causes carrier to release 2 K⁺ inside the cell.

Sodium-Potassium Pump
Figure 6.11

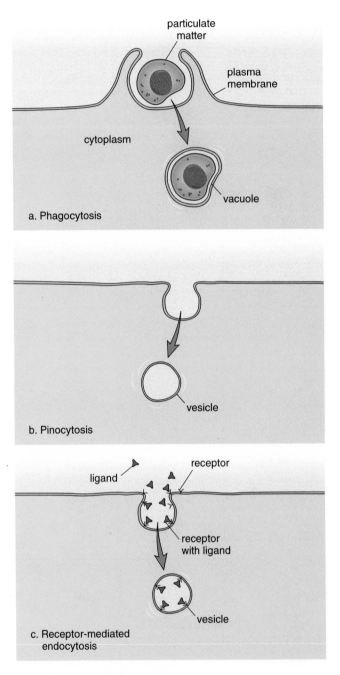

Three Methods of Endocytosis
Figure 6.12

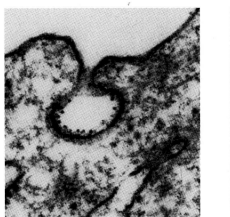

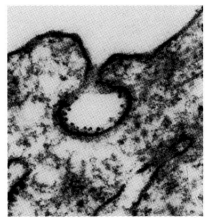

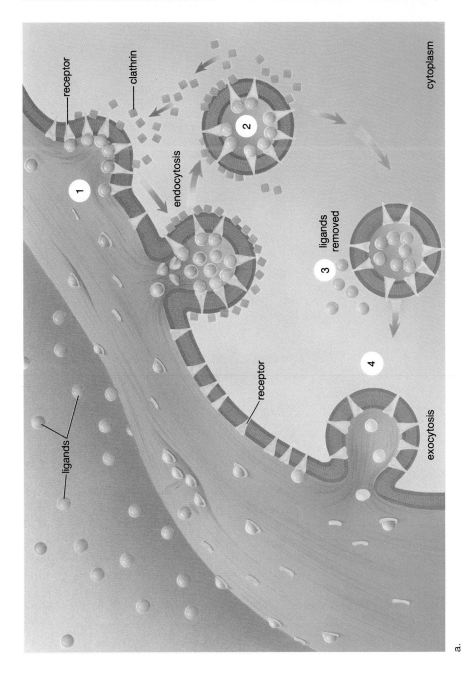

b.

a.

Receptor-Mediated Endocytosis
Figure 6.13

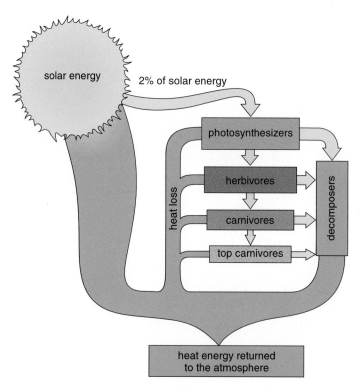

Loss of Useful Energy in Ecosystem
Figure 7.2

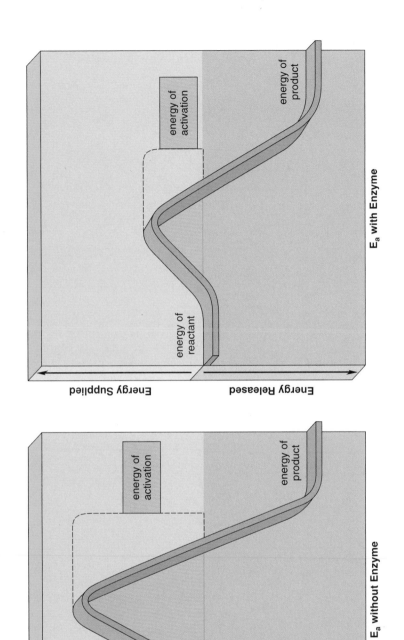

Energy of Activation
Figure 7.3

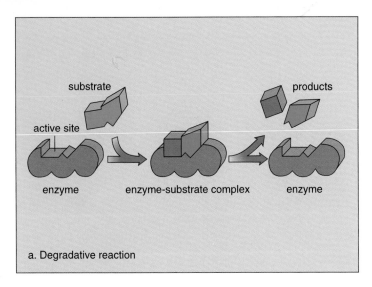

a. Degradative reaction

Enzymatic Action
Figure 7.4a

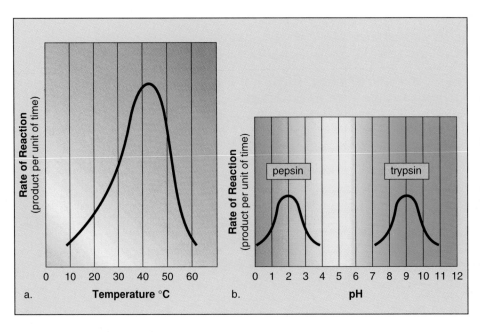

Rate of Enzymatic Reaction
Figure 7.5

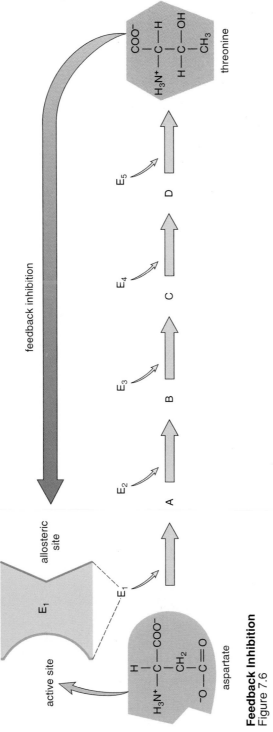

Feedback Inhibition
Figure 7.6

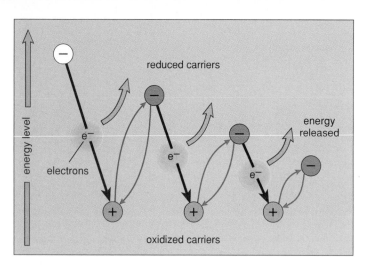

Electron Transport System
Figure 7.7

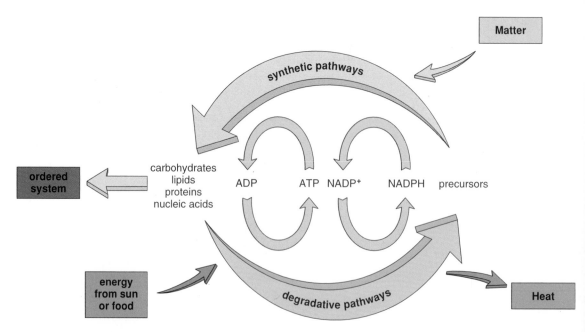

Metabolic Reactions
Figure 7.8

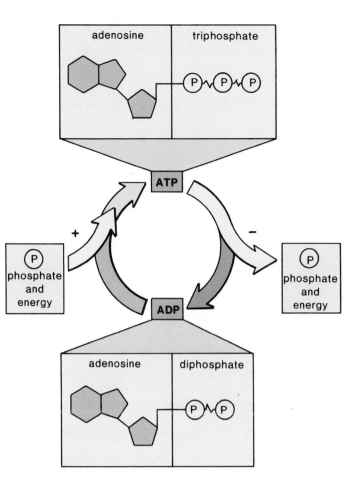

ATP Cycle
Figure 7.9

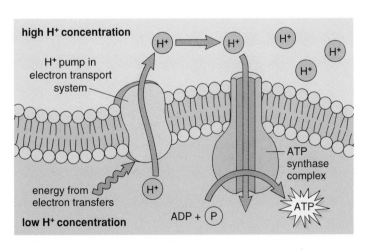

Chemiosmotic ATP Synthesis
Figure 7.10

33

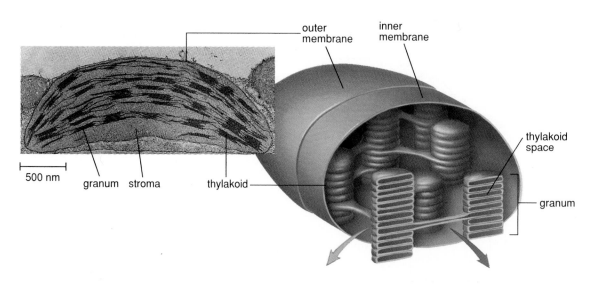

outer membrane

inner membrane

thylakoid space

granum

granum   stroma

thylakoid

500 nm

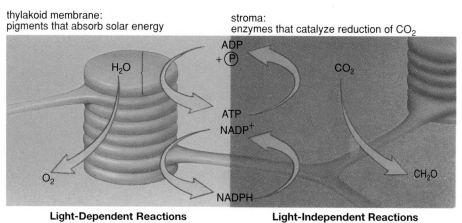

thylakoid membrane:
pigments that absorb solar energy

stroma:
enzymes that catalyze reduction of CO_2

H_2O

O_2

ADP
$+ \text{P}$

ATP

$NADP^+$

NADPH

CO_2

CH_2O

Light-Dependent Reactions

Light-Independent Reactions

Chloroplast Structure and Function
Figure 8.3

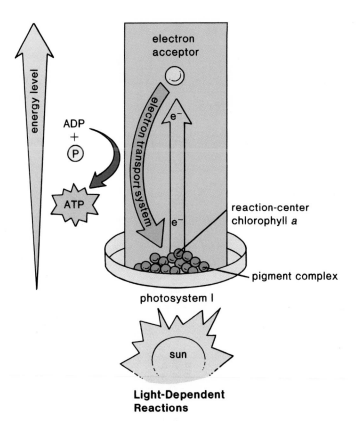

Cyclic Electron Pathway
Figure 8.5

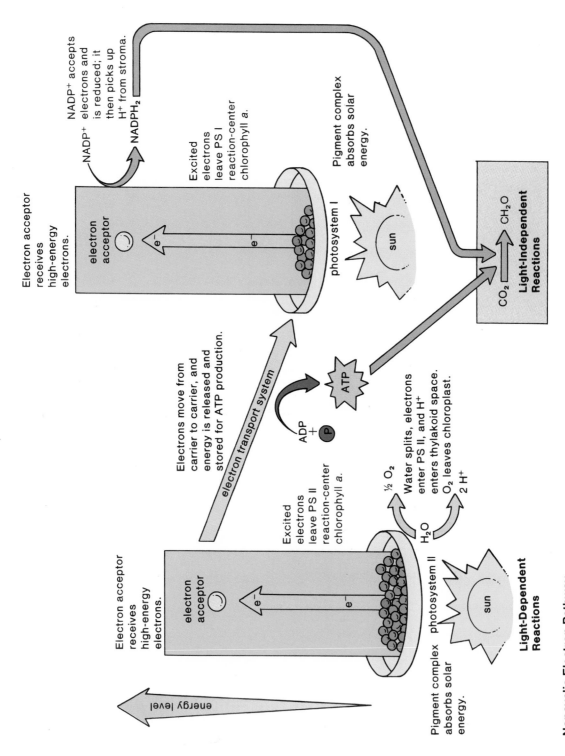

Noncyclic Electron Pathway
Figure 8.6

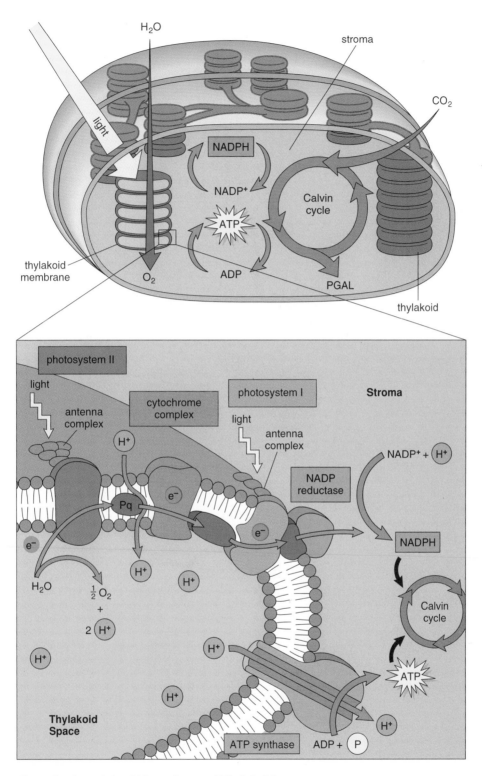

Organization of the Chloroplast and Thylakoid
Figure 8.7

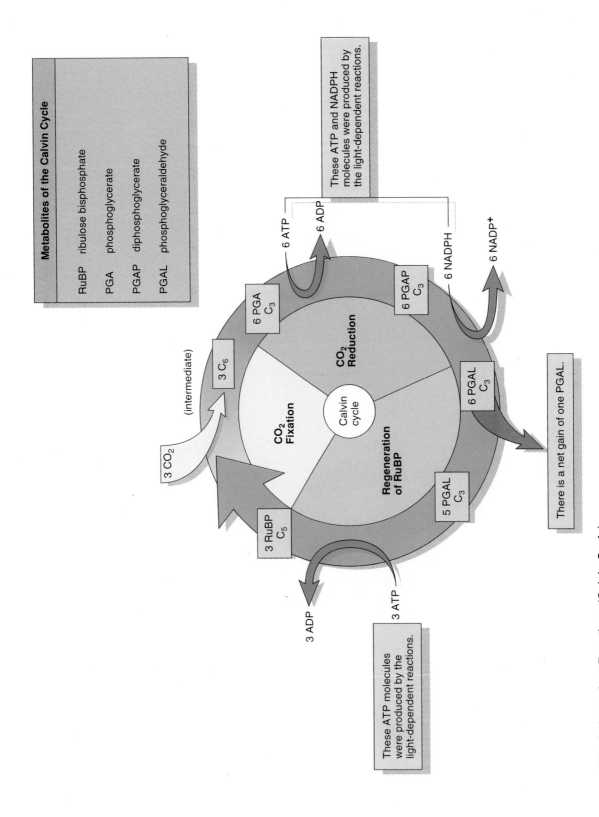

Metabolites of the Calvin Cycle

RuBP   ribulose bisphosphate
PGA   phosphoglycerate
PGAP   diphosphoglycerate
PGAL   phosphoglyceraldehyde

These ATP and NADPH molecules were produced by the light-dependent reactions.

6 ATP
6 ADP
6 NADPH
6 NADP$^+$

6 PGA
C_3
6 PGAP
C_3

3 C_6
(intermediate)

CO$_2$ Reduction

CO$_2$ Fixation

Calvin cycle

Regeneration of RuBP

3 CO$_2$

3 RuBP
C_5

6 PGAL
C_3

5 PGAL
C_3

There is a net gain of one PGAL.

3 ADP
3 ATP

These ATP molecules were produced by the light-dependent reactions.

Light-Independent Reactions (Calvin Cycle)
Figure 8.9

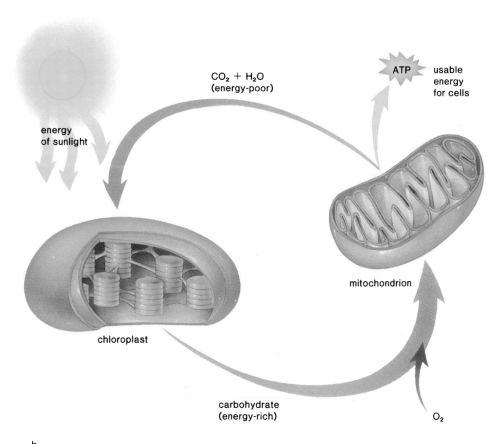

CO$_2$ + H$_2$O
(energy-poor)

ATP   usable
             energy
             for cells

energy
of sunlight

mitochondrion

chloroplast

carbohydrate
(energy-rich)

O$_2$

b.

Respiration/Photosynthesis Relationship
Figure 9.1*b*

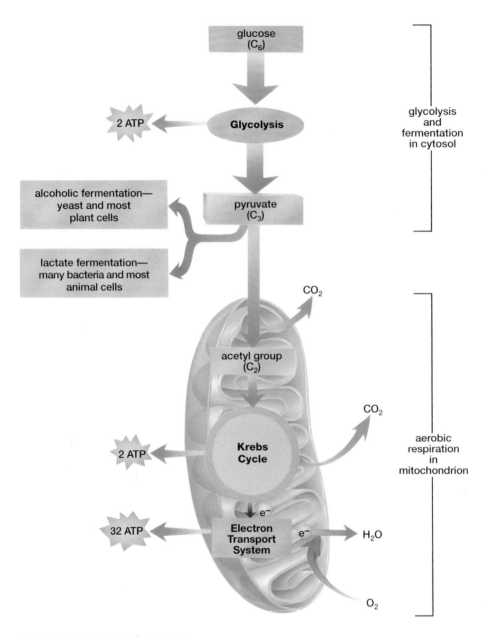

Cellular Respiration Overview
Figure 9.2

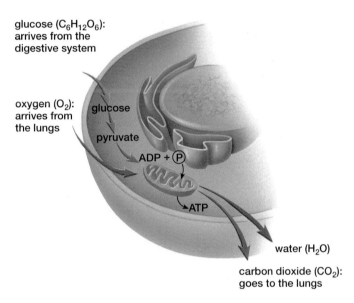

glucose ($C_6H_{12}O_6$):
arrives from the
digestive system

oxygen (O_2):
arrives from
the lungs

glucose

pyruvate

ADP + Ⓟ

ATP

water (H_2O)

carbon dioxide (CO_2):
goes to the lungs

Aerobic Respiration in the Body
Figure 9.3

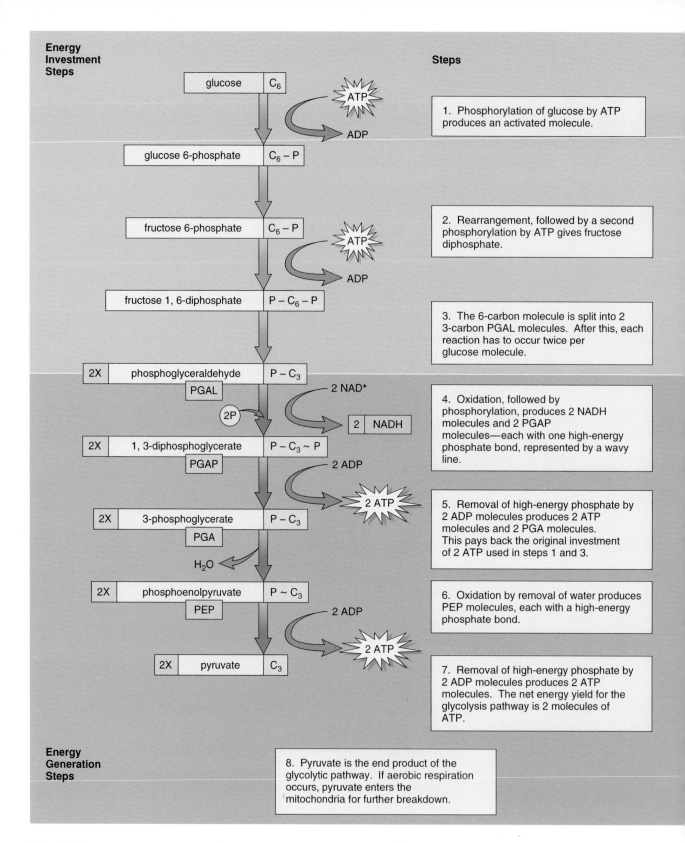

Glycolysis
Figure 9.4

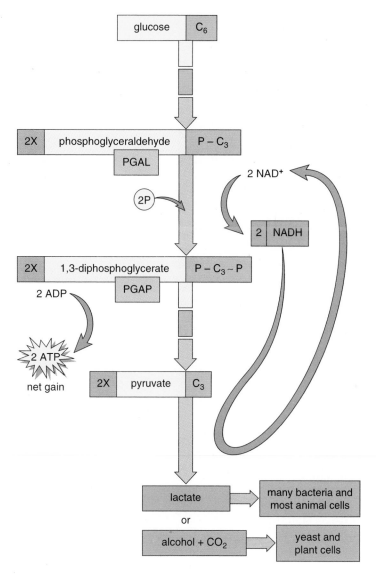

Fermentation
Figure 9.5

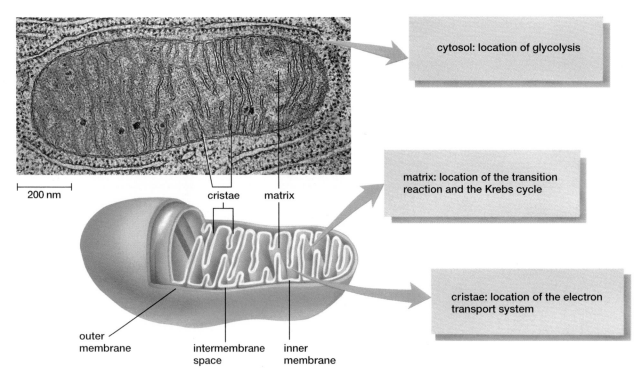

cristae   matrix

200 nm

cytosol: location of glycolysis

matrix: location of the transition reaction and the Krebs cycle

cristae: location of the electron transport system

outer membrane

intermembrane space

inner membrane

Mitochondrion Structure and Function
Figure 9.6

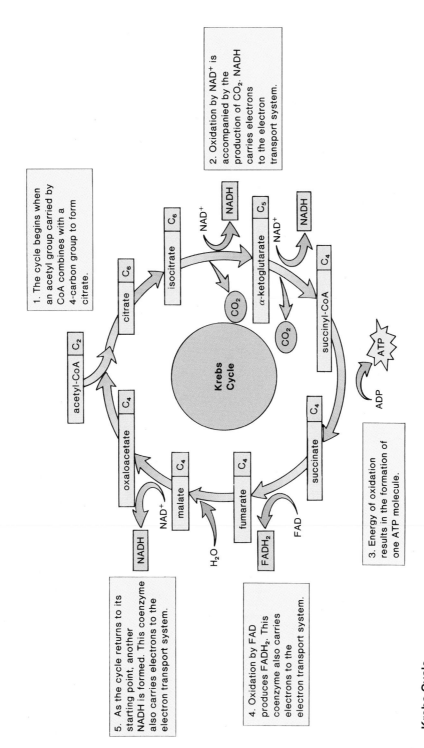

Krebs Cycle
Figure 9.7

45

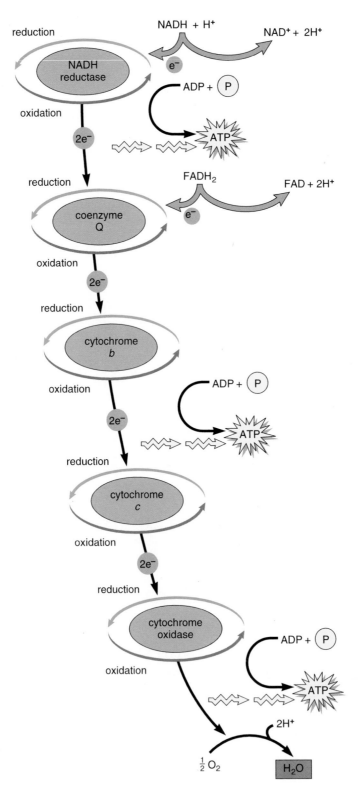

Electron Transport System
Figure 9.8

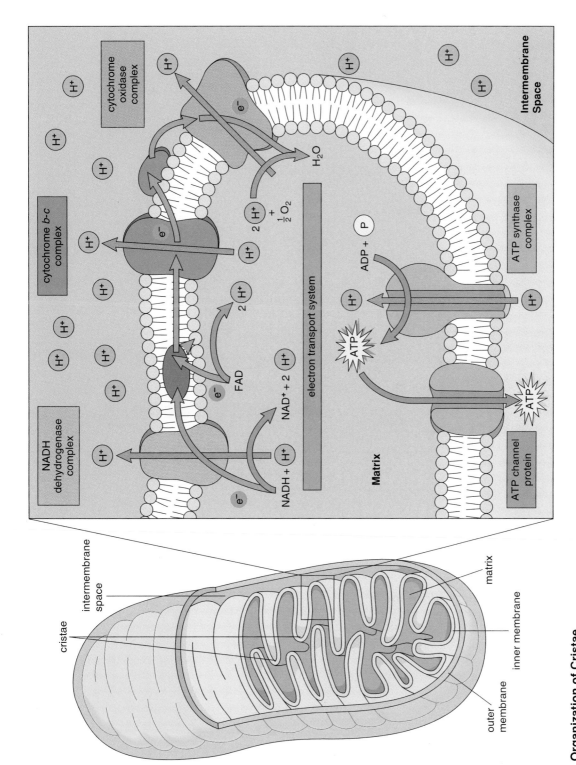

Organization of Cristae
Figure 9.9

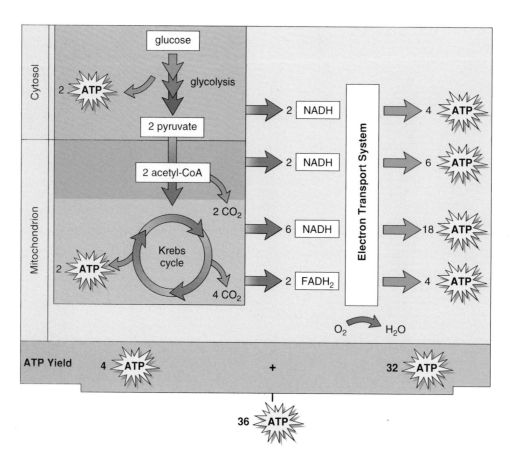

Summary of Glucose Breakdown
Figure 9.10

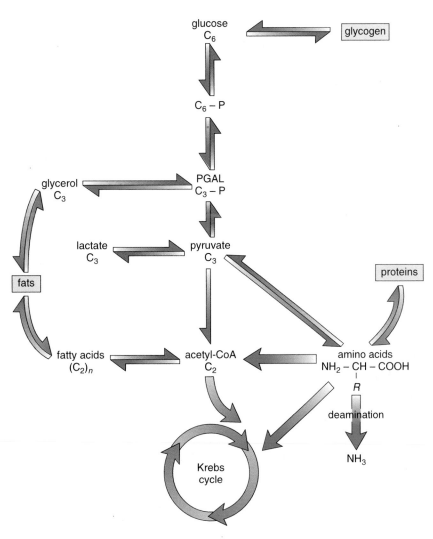

Metabolic Pool Concept
Figure 9.11

Stage	Main Events	Length of time (hours)	
		Vicia faba	*Homo sapiens* (cultured fibroblasts)
G_1	Organelles begin to double in number	4.9	6.3
S	Replication of DNA	7.5	7.0
G_2	Synthesis of proteins	4.9	2.0
M	Mitosis	2.0	0.7
	Total:	19.3	16.0

Interphase

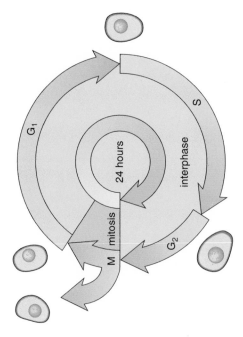

Cell Cycle
Figure 10.3

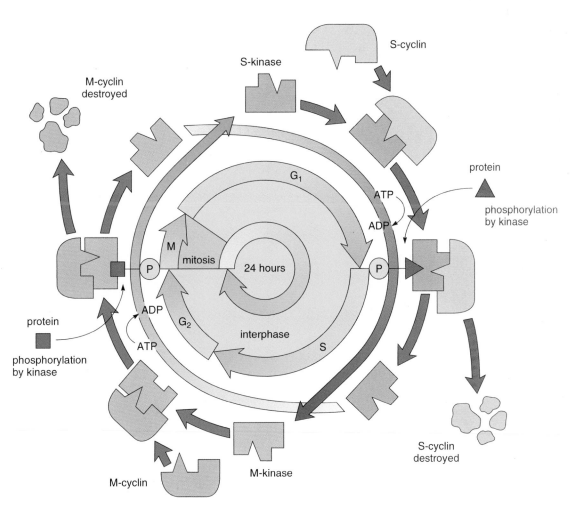

Control of Cell Cycle
Figure 10.4

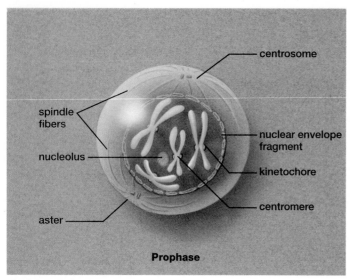
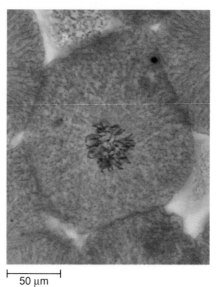

centrosome

spindle fibers

nucleolus

aster

nuclear envelope fragment

kinetochore

centromere

Prophase

50 μm

Prophase (Animal Cell)
Figure 10.5

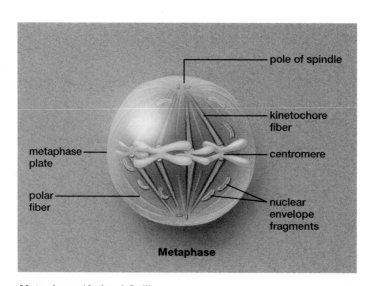
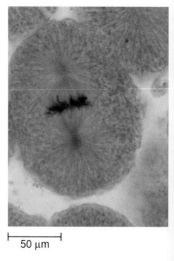

pole of spindle

kinetochore fiber

centromere

metaphase plate

polar fiber

nuclear envelope fragments

Metaphase

50 μm

Metaphase (Animal Cell)
Figure 10.6

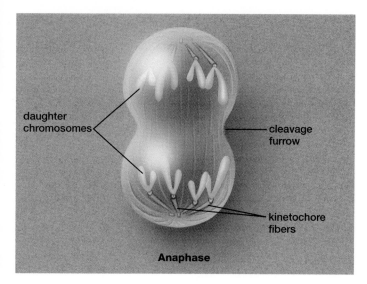
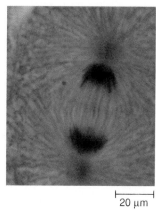

daughter chromosomes

cleavage furrow

kinetochore fibers

Anaphase

20 µm

Anaphase (Animal Cell)
Figure 10.7

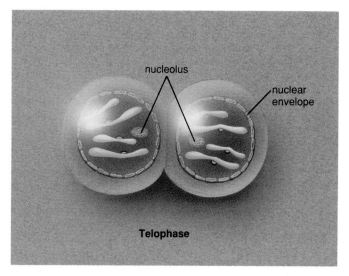
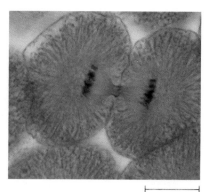

nucleolus

nuclear envelope

Telophase

50 µm

Telophase (Animal Cell)
Figure 10.8

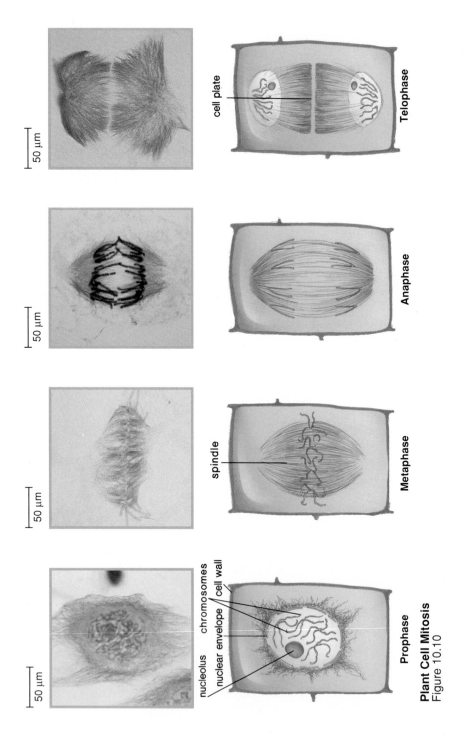

Plant Cell Mitosis
Figure 10.10

Prophase · nucleolus · nuclear envelope · chromosomes · cell wall

Metaphase · spindle

Anaphase

Telophase · cell plate

50 μm

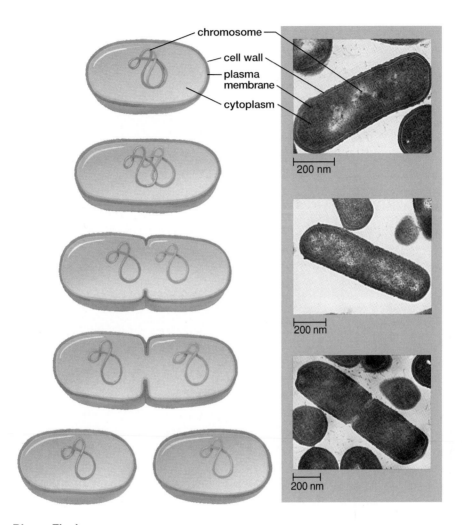

chromosome

cell wall

plasma membrane

cytoplasm

200 nm

200 nm

200 nm

Binary Fission
Figure 10.11

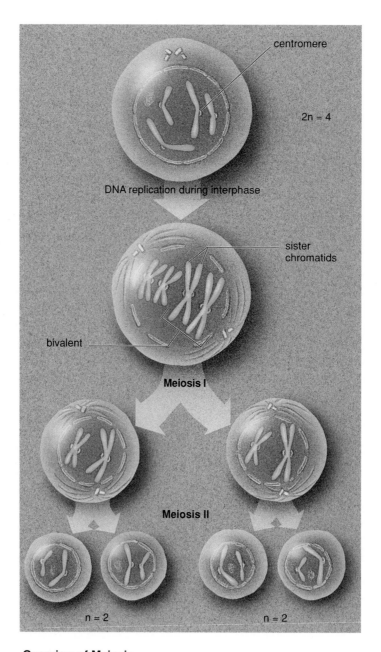

Overview of Meiosis
Figure 11.2

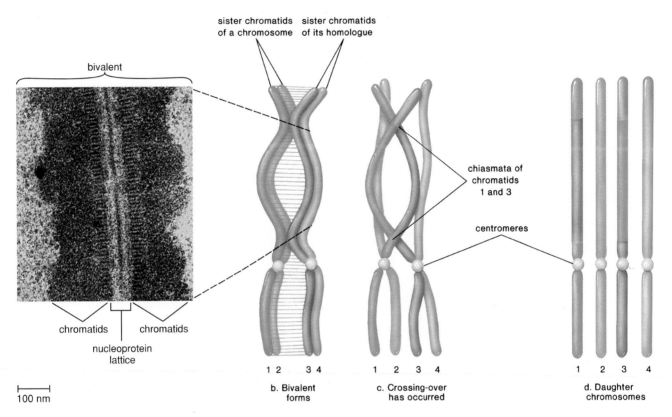

sister chromatids of a chromosome   sister chromatids of its homologue

bivalent

chromatids   chromatids

nucleoprotein lattice

100 nm

chiasmata of chromatids 1 and 3

centromeres

1 2   3 4
b. Bivalent forms

1   2   3   4
c. Crossing-over has occurred

1   2   3   4
d. Daughter chromosomes

Crossing-Over During Meiosis I
Figure 11.3

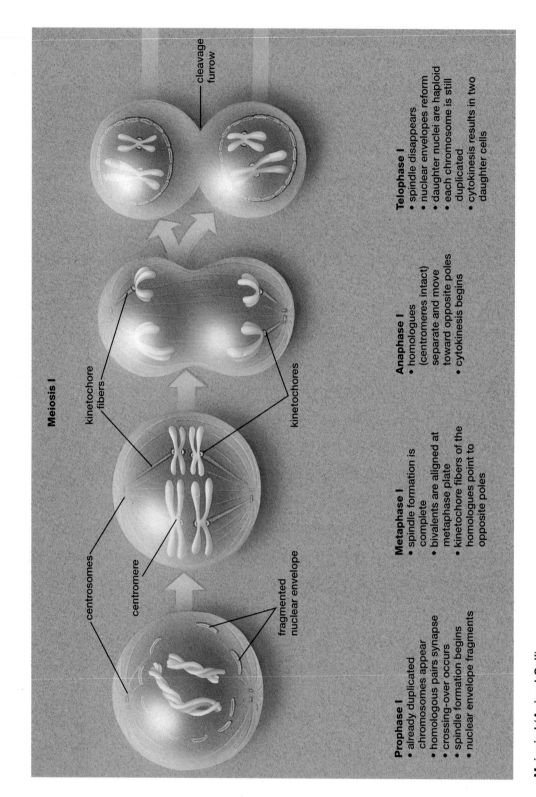

Meiosis I

cleavage furrow

kinetochore fibers

kinetochores

centrosomes

centromere

fragmented nuclear envelope

Prophase I
- already duplicated chromosomes appear
- homologous pairs synapse
- crossing-over occurs
- spindle formation begins
- nuclear envelope fragments

Metaphase I
- spindle formation is complete
- bivalents are aligned at metaphase plate
- kinetochore fibers of the homologues point to opposite poles

Anaphase I
- homologues (centromeres intact) separate and move toward opposite poles
- cytokinesis begins

Telophase I
- spindle disappears
- nuclear envelopes reform
- daughter nuclei are haploid
- each chromosome is still duplicated
- cytokinesis results in two daughter cells

Meiosis I (Animal Cell)
Figure 11.5

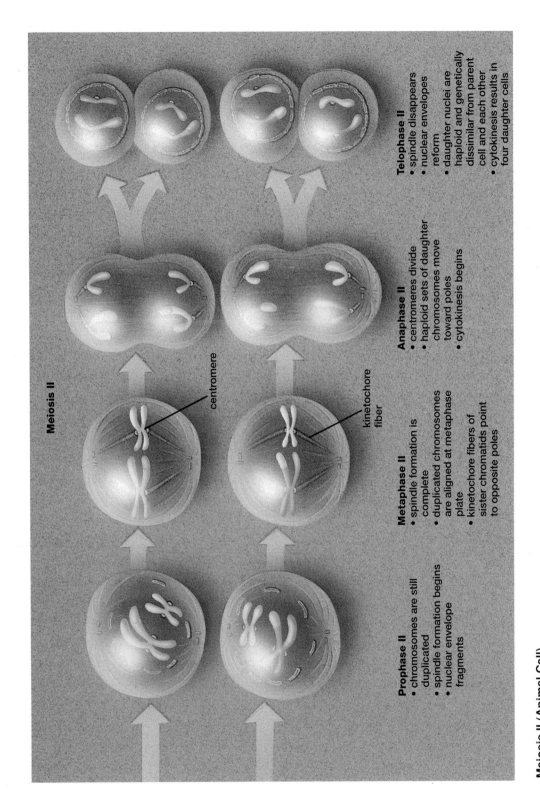

Meiosis II

Prophase II
- chromosomes are still duplicated
- spindle formation begins
- nuclear envelope fragments

centromere

Metaphase II
- spindle formation is complete
- duplicated chromosomes are aligned at metaphase plate
- kinetochore fibers of sister chromatids point to opposite poles

kinetochore fiber

Anaphase II
- centromeres divide
- haploid sets of daughter chromosomes move toward poles
- cytokinesis begins

Telophase II
- spindle disappears
- nuclear envelopes reform
- daughter nuclei are haploid and genetically dissimilar from parent cell and each other
- cytokinesis results in four daughter cells

Meiosis II (Animal Cell)
Figure 11.5

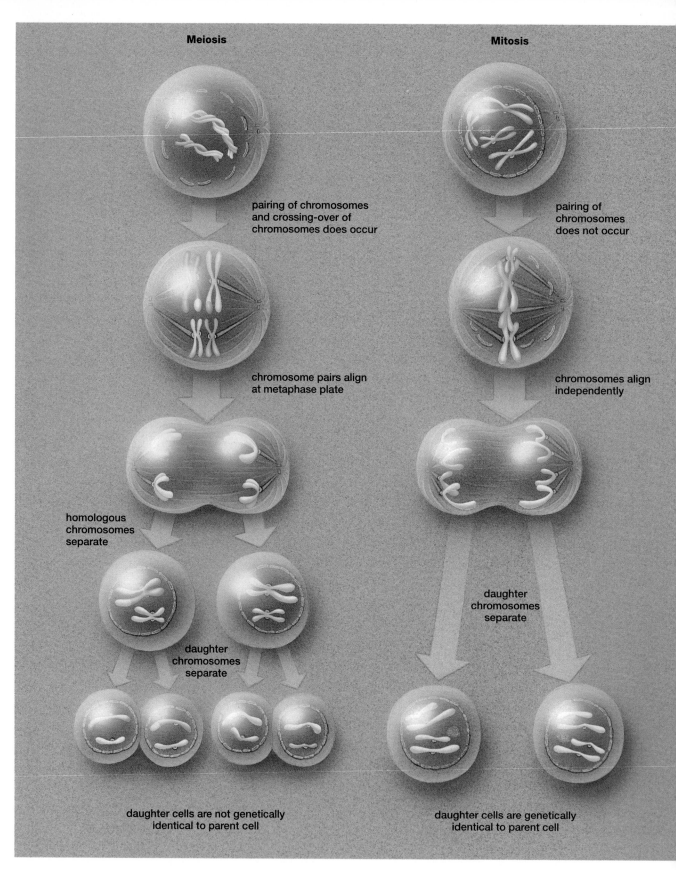

Meiosis

Mitosis

pairing of chromosomes and crossing-over of chromosomes does occur

pairing of chromosomes does not occur

chromosome pairs align at metaphase plate

chromosomes align independently

homologous chromosomes separate

daughter chromosomes separate

daughter chromosomes separate

daughter cells are not genetically identical to parent cell

daughter cells are genetically identical to parent cell

Comparison of Meiosis and Mitosis
Figure 11.7

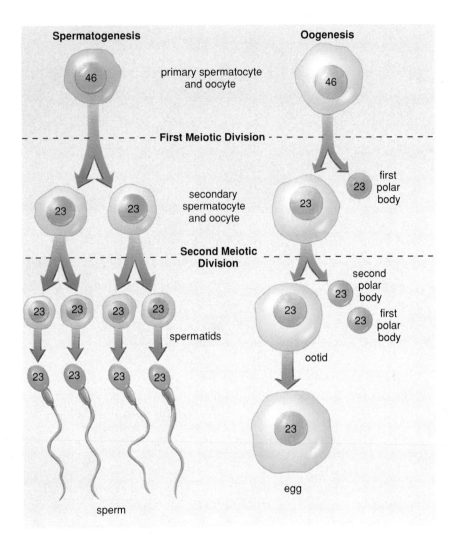

Spermatogenesis and Oogenesis in Mammals
Figure 11.8

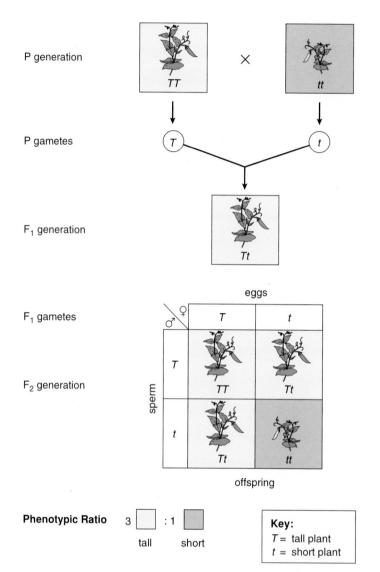

P generation

P gametes

F₁ generation

F₁ gametes

F₂ generation

eggs

offspring

Phenotypic Ratio 3 ☐ : 1 ▨

tall   short

Key:
T = tall plant
t = short plant

Monohybrid Cross
Figure 12.3

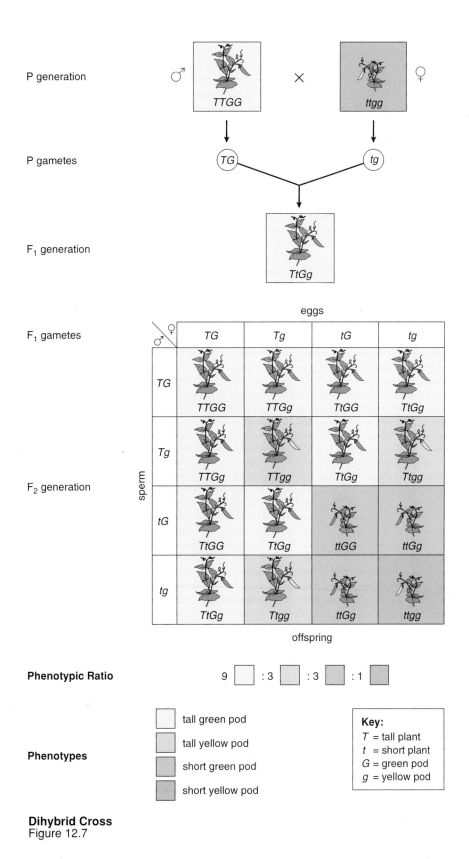

P generation

P gametes

F₁ generation

F₁ gametes

F₂ generation

Phenotypic Ratio

9 : 3 : 3 : 1

Phenotypes

tall green pod

tall yellow pod

short green pod

short yellow pod

Key:
T = tall plant
t = short plant
G = green pod
g = yellow pod

Dihybrid Cross
Figure 12.7

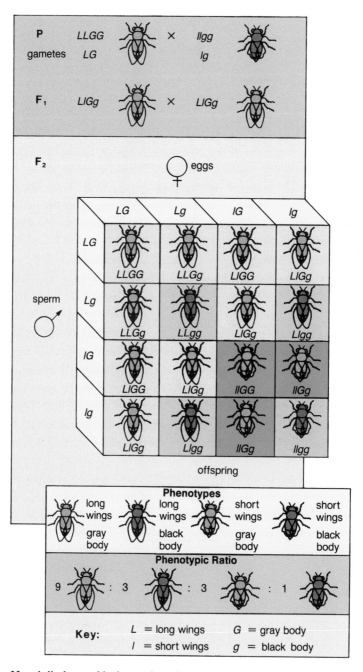

Mendel's Law of Independent Assortment
Figure 12.8

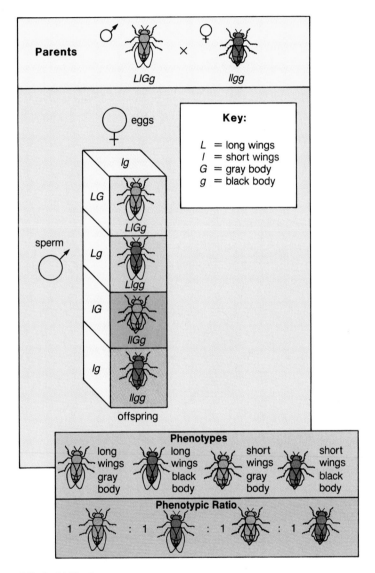

Dihybrid Testcross
Figure 12.9

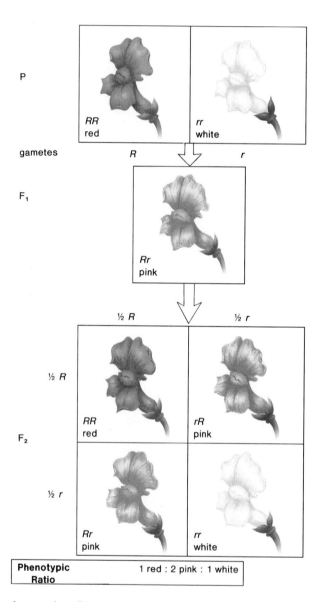

P

gametes

F₁

F₂

RR
red

rr
white

R

r

Rr
pink

½ R

½ r

½ R

½ r

RR
red

rR
pink

Rr
pink

rr
white

Phenotypic Ratio	1 red : 2 pink : 1 white

Incomplete Dominance
Figure 13.1

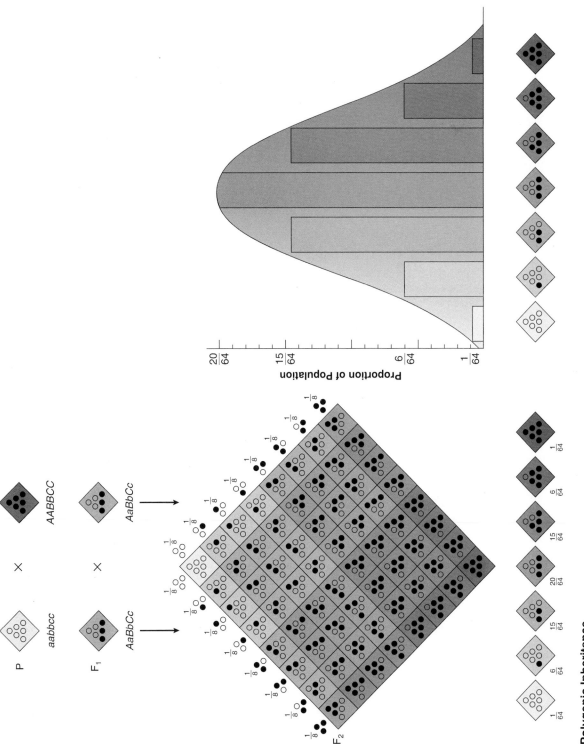

Polygenic Inheritance
Figure 13.5

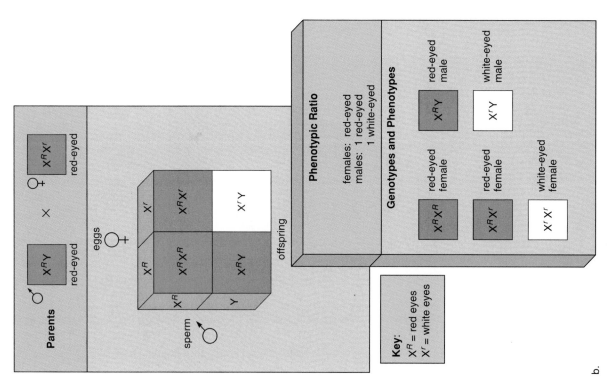

Parents

♂ X^R Y   ×   ♀ X^R X^r
red-eyed   red-eyed

eggs ♀

	X^R	X^r
sperm ♂ X^R	X^R X^R	X^R X^r
Y	X^R Y	X^r Y

offspring

Phenotypic Ratio

females: red-eyed
males: 1 red-eyed
1 white-eyed

Genotypes and Phenotypes

X^R X^R red-eyed female	X^R X^r red-eyed female	X^r X^r white-eyed female

X^R Y red-eyed male	X^r Y white-eyed male

Key:
X^R = red eyes
X^r = white eyes

b.

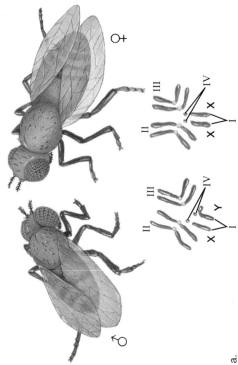

♀

III
II
X
I
IV
X

♂

III
II
X
IV
Y
I

a.

***Drosphila* Cross**
Figure 13.6

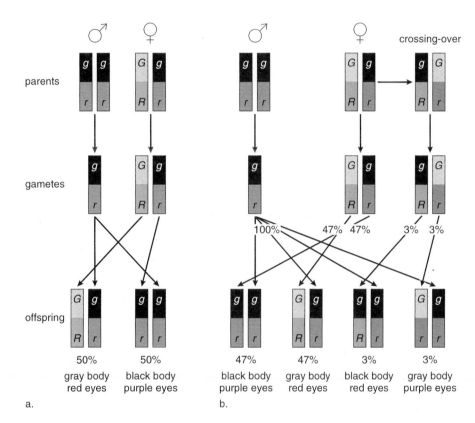

Key:

G = gray body
g = black body
R = red eyes
r = purple eyes

parents

gametes

offspring

crossing-over

50%

gray body
red eyes

50%

black body
purple eyes

a.

47%

black body
purple eyes

47%

gray body
red eyes

3%

black body
red eyes

3%

gray body
purple eyes

b.

100%   47% 47%   3%   3%

Complete v. Incomplete Linkage
Figure 13.7

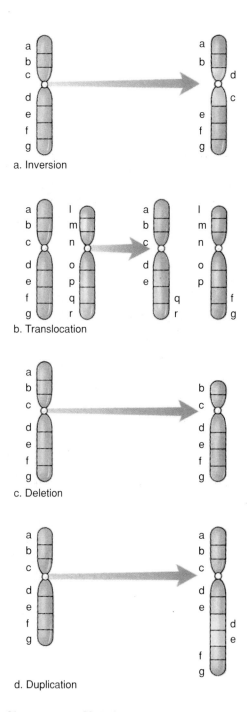

a. Inversion

b. Translocation

c. Deletion

d. Duplication

Chromosome Mutations
Figure 13.10

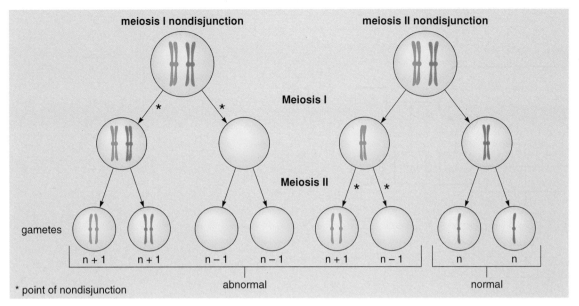

a.

Nondisjunction
Figure 14.2*a*

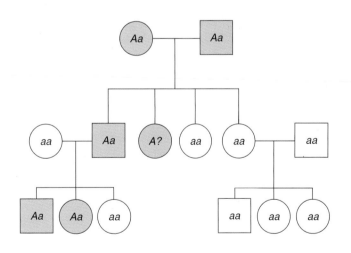

Key:

AA = affected
Aa = affected
aa = normal

a.

Autosomal Dominant Disorder Pedigree Chart
Figure 14.6*a*

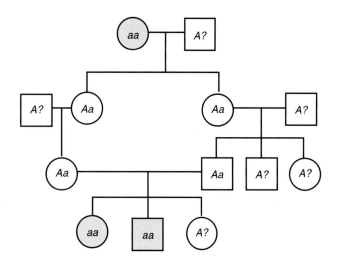

Key:
aa = affected
Aa = carrier (appears normal)
AA = normal

a.

Autosomal Recessive Disorder Pedigree Chart
Figure 14.7*a*

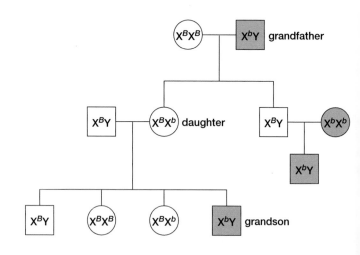

Key:
X^BX^B = normal female X^BY = normal male
X^BX^b = carrier female X^bY = color-blind male
X^bX^b = color-blind female

a.

X-linked Recessive Disorder Pedigree Chart
Figure 14.13*a*

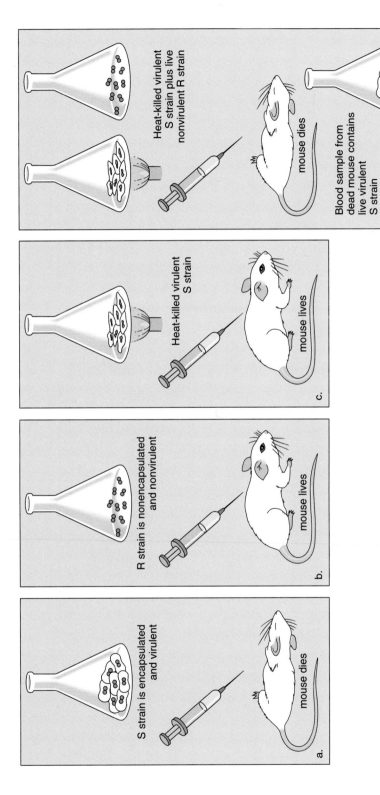

S strain is encapsulated and virulent

mouse dies

a.

R strain is nonencapsulated and nonvirulent

mouse lives

b.

Heat-killed virulent S strain

mouse lives

c.

Heat-killed virulent S strain plus live nonvirulent R strain

mouse dies

Blood sample from dead mouse contains live virulent S strain

d.

Griffith's Transformation Experiment
Figure 15.1

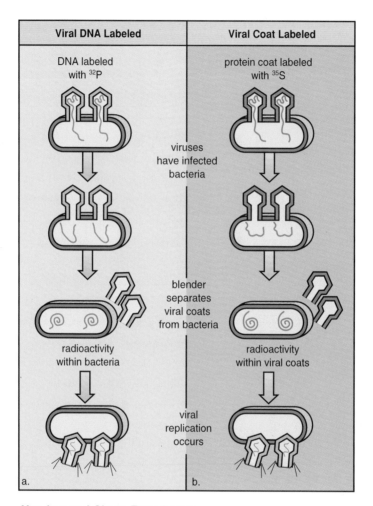

Viral DNA Labeled

DNA labeled
with ^{32}P

Viral Coat Labeled

protein coat labeled
with ^{35}S

viruses
have infected
bacteria

blender
separates
viral coats
from bacteria

radioactivity
within bacteria

radioactivity
within viral coats

viral
replication
occurs

a.

b.

Hershey and Chase Experiment
Figure 15.3

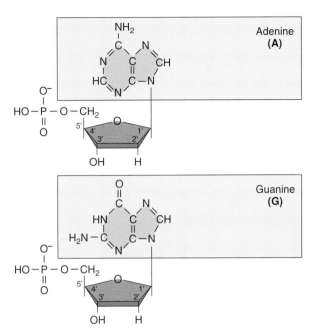

a. **Purine Nucleotides**

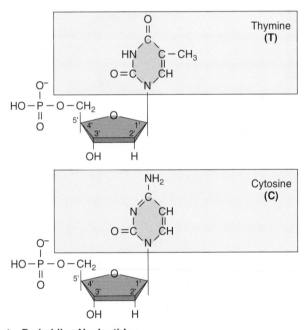

b. **Pyrimidine Nucleotides**

Chargaff's DNA Data: Base Composition in Various Species (%)				
Species	**A**	**T**	**G**	**C**
Homo sapiens	31.0	31.5	19.1	18.4
Drosophila melanogaster	27.3	27.6	22.5	22.5
Zea mays	25.6	25.3	24.5	24.6
Neurospora crassa	23.0	23.3	27.1	26.6
Escherichia coli	24.6	24.3	25.5	25.6
Bacillus subtilis	28.4	29.0	21.0	21.6

c.

Nucleotide Composition of DNA
Figure 15.4

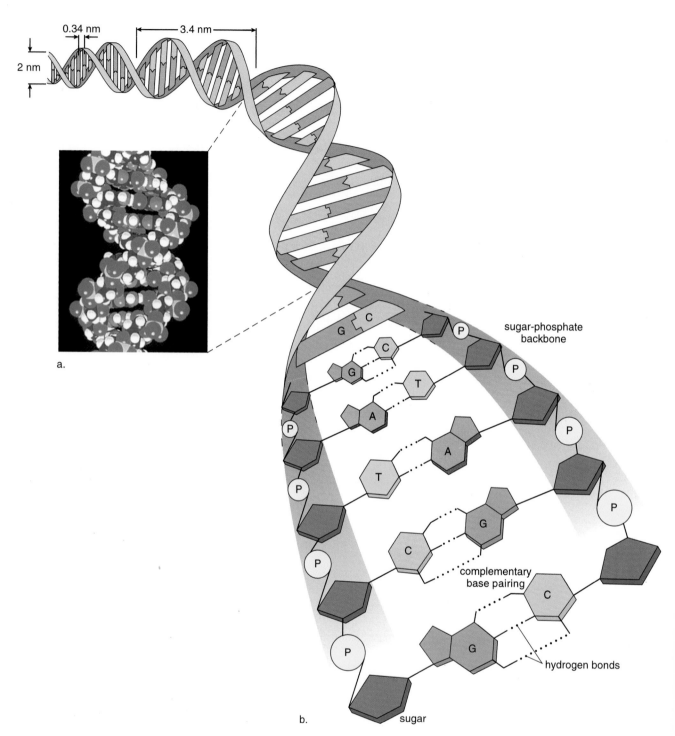

0.34 nm

3.4 nm

2 nm

a.

sugar-phosphate backbone

P

P

P

P

P

P

P

P

P

G C

C

G

T

A

A

T

G

C

complementary base pairing

C

G

hydrogen bonds

b.

sugar

Watson and Crick Model of DNA
Figure 15.6

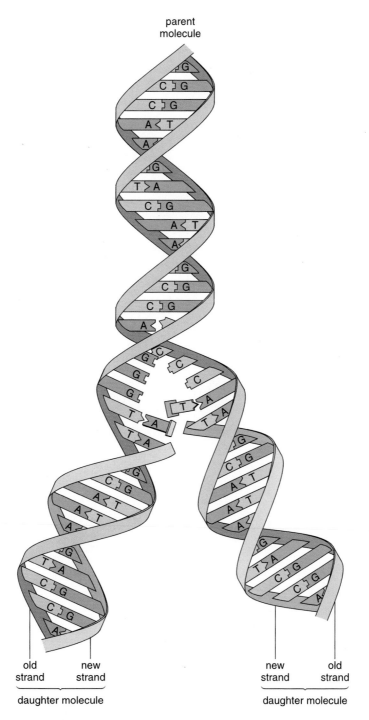

parent
molecule

old
strand

new
strand

daughter molecule

new
strand

old
strand

daughter molecule

Semiconservative Replication
Figure 15.7

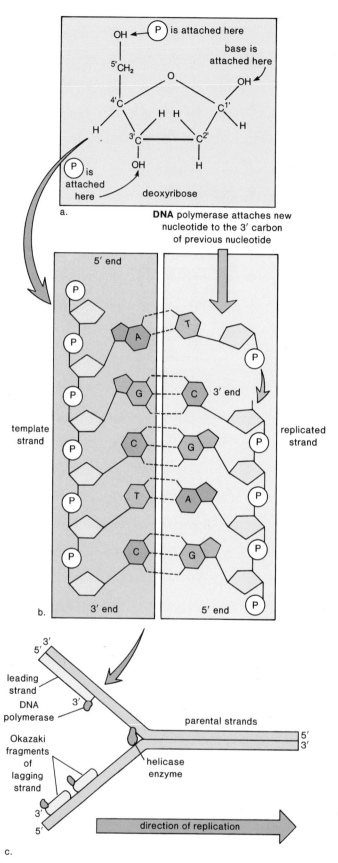

a.

(P) is attached here

base is attached here

5'CH₂

O

4'C

3'C

C2'

C1'

H

H

H

H

H

OH

OH

OH

(P) is attached here

deoxyribose

DNA polymerase attaches new nucleotide to the 3' carbon of previous nucleotide

b.

5' end

template strand

replicated strand

3' end

3' end

5' end

P A — T P

P G --- C 3' end P

P C --- G P

P T --- A P

P C --- G P

P

c.

5' 3'

leading strand

DNA polymerase 3'

Okazaki fragments of lagging strand

3'

5'

helicase enzyme

parental strands 5' 3'

direction of replication

DNA Replication (In Depth)
Figure 15A

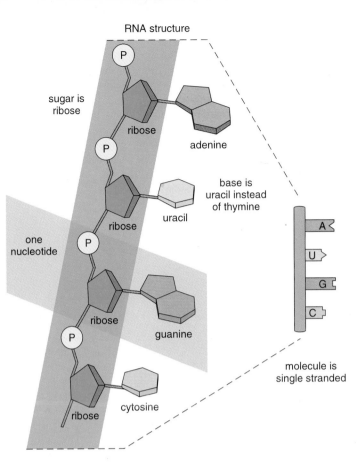

RNA Structure
Figure 16.3

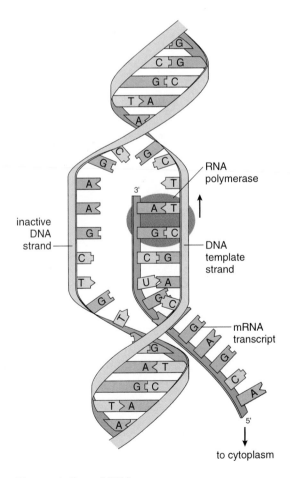

Transcription of DNA
Figure 16.5

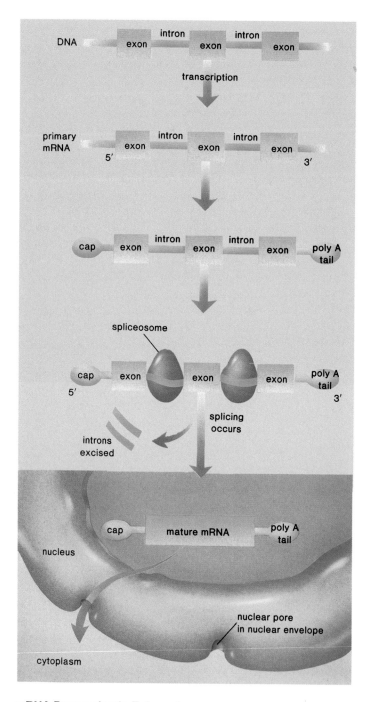

mRNA Processing in Eukaryotes
Figure 16.7

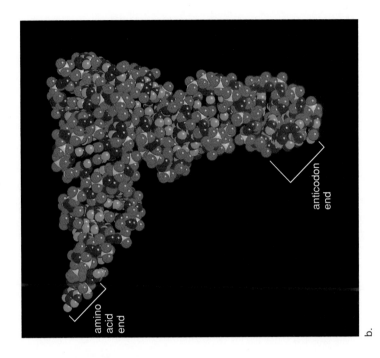

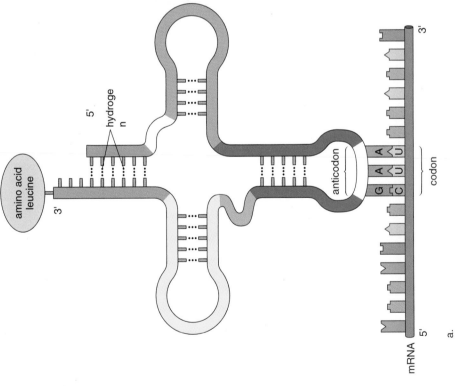

Structure of tRNA Molecule
Figure 16.9

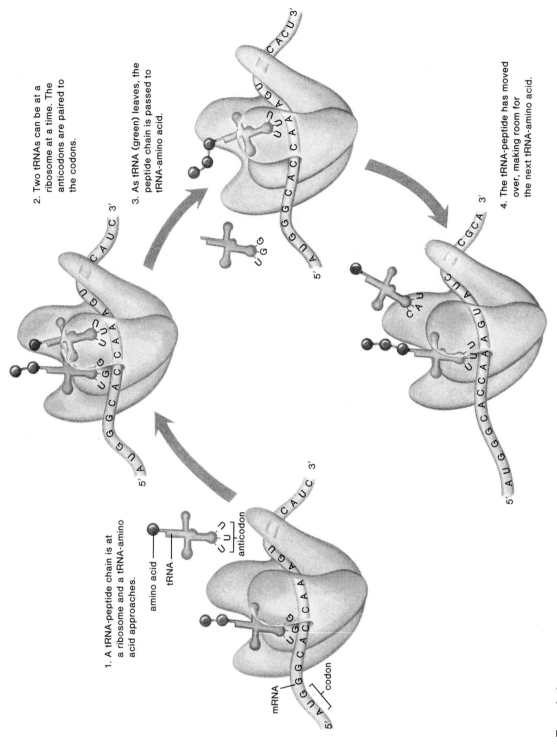

2. Two tRNAs can be at a ribosome at a time. The anticodons are paired to the codons.

3. As tRNA (green) leaves, the peptide chain is passed to tRNA-amino acid.

4. The tRNA-peptide has moved over, making room for the next tRNA-amino acid.

1. A tRNA-peptide chain is at a ribosome and a tRNA-amino acid approaches.

amino acid
tRNA
anticodon

mRNA
codon

Translation
Figure 16.10

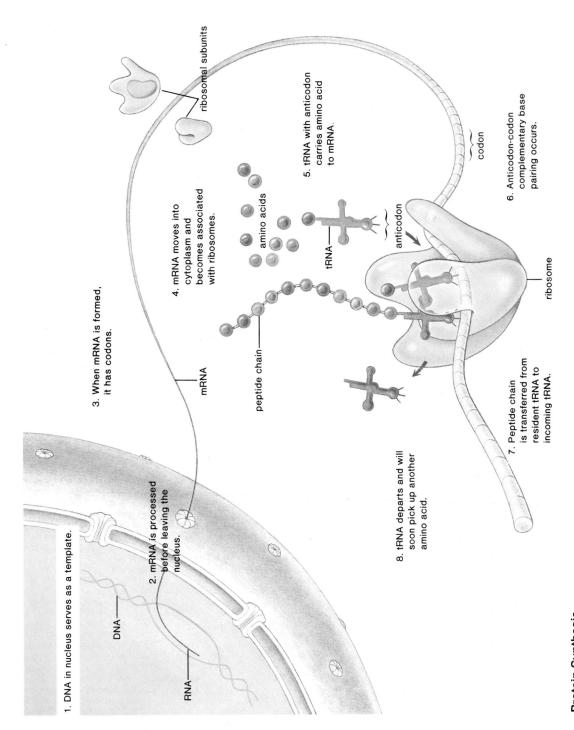

1. DNA in nucleus serves as a template.

DNA

2. mRNA is processed before leaving the nucleus.

RNA

3. When mRNA is formed, it has codons.

mRNA

4. mRNA moves into cytoplasm and becomes associated with ribosomes.

ribosomal subunits

amino acids

5. tRNA with anticodon carries amino acid to mRNA.

tRNA

anticodon

codon

6. Anticodon-codon complementary base pairing occurs.

peptide chain

ribosome

7. Peptide chain is transferred from resident tRNA to incoming tRNA.

8. tRNA departs and will soon pick up another amino acid.

Protein Synthesis
Figure 16.11

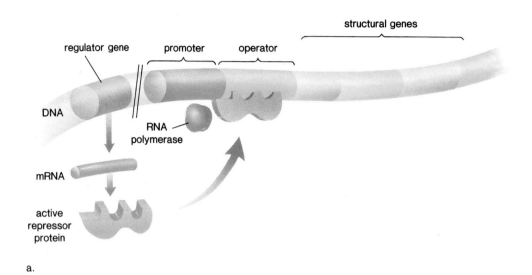

a.

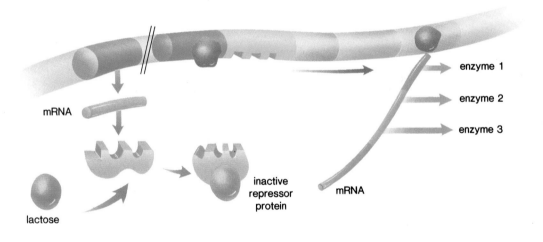

b.

Lac **Operon**
Figure 17.1

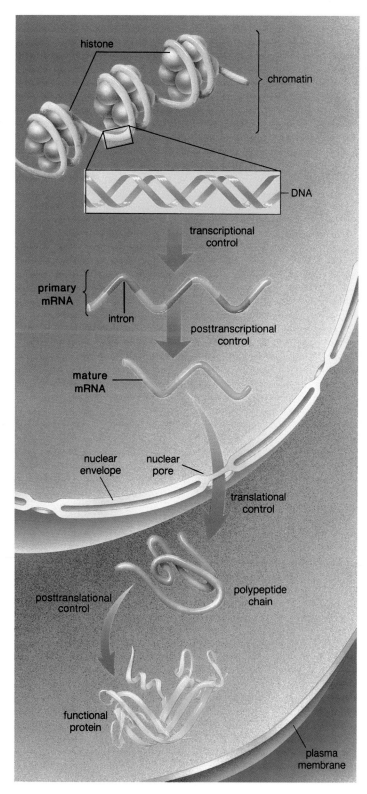

Levels of Control of Gene Expression
Figure 17.2

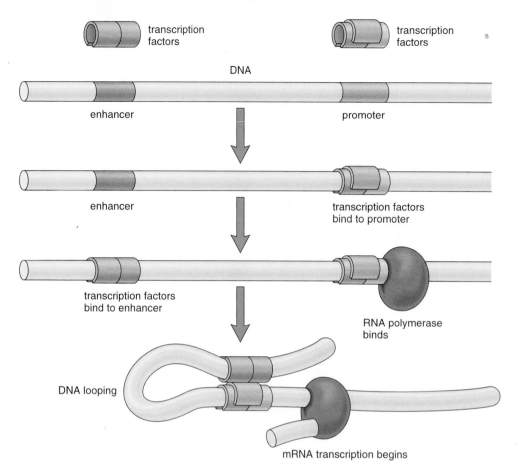

Transcription Factors
Figure 17.6

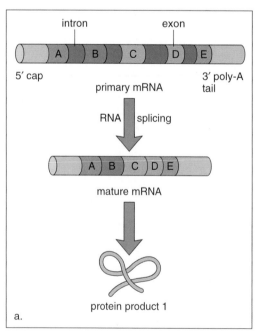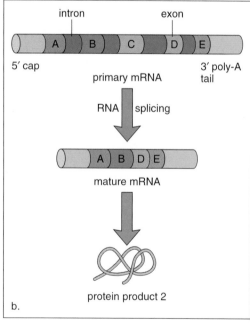

Alternative Splicing of mRNA Transcripts
Figure 17.7

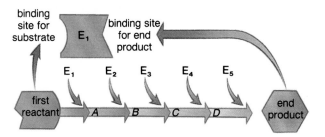

Posttranslational Control
Figure 17.8

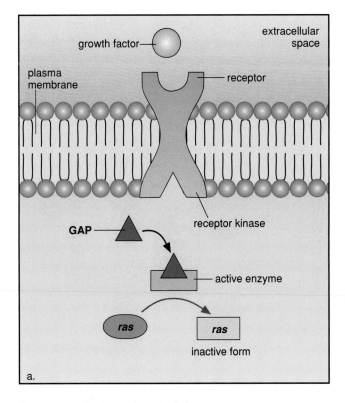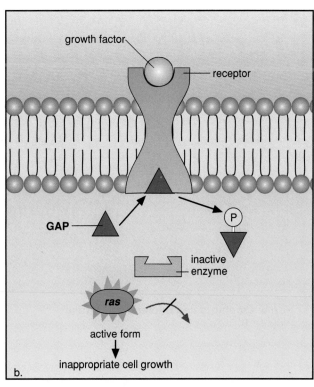

Regulatory Pathway/*ras* Protein
Figure 17.11

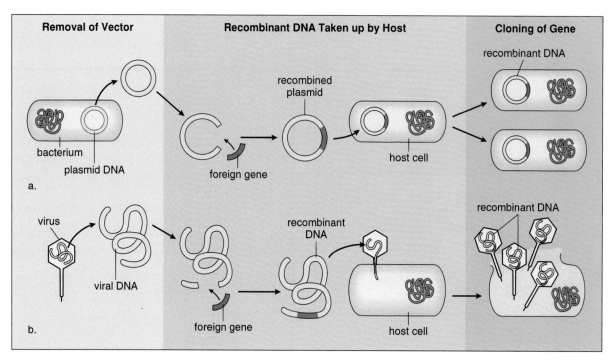

Removal of Vector **Recombinant DNA Taken up by Host** **Cloning of Gene**

recombinant DNA

bacterium

plasmid DNA

recombined plasmid

host cell

foreign gene

a.

virus

viral DNA

recombinant DNA

foreign gene

host cell

recombinant DNA

b.

Gene Cloning Using Bacteria and Viruses
Figure 18.1

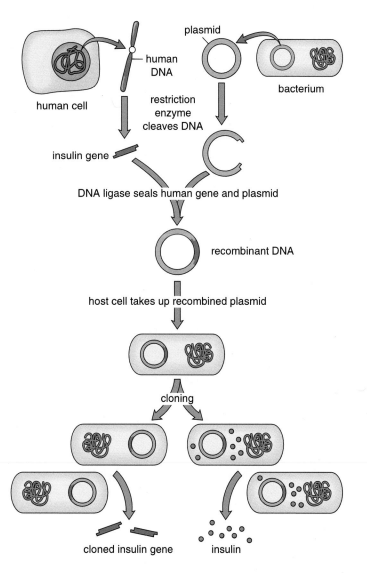

human cell

human DNA

plasmid

bacterium

restriction enzyme cleaves DNA

insulin gene

DNA ligase seals human gene and plasmid

recombinant DNA

host cell takes up recombined plasmid

cloning

cloned insulin gene

insulin

Cloning of a Human Gene
Figure 18.2

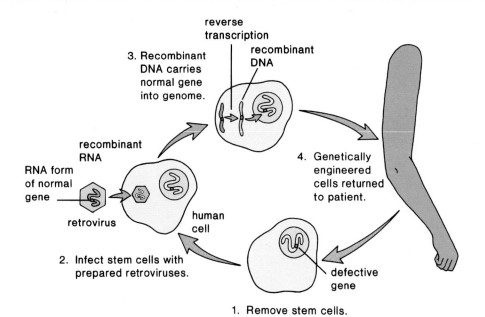

3. Recombinant DNA carries normal gene into genome.

reverse transcription

recombinant DNA

recombinant RNA

RNA form of normal gene

retrovirus

human cell

4. Genetically engineered cells returned to patient.

2. Infect stem cells with prepared retroviruses.

defective gene

1. Remove stem cells.

Ex vivo Gene Therapy In Humans
Figure 18.8

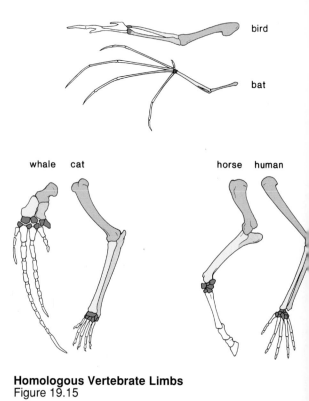

bird

bat

whale   cat   horse human

Homologous Vertebrate Limbs
Figure 19.15

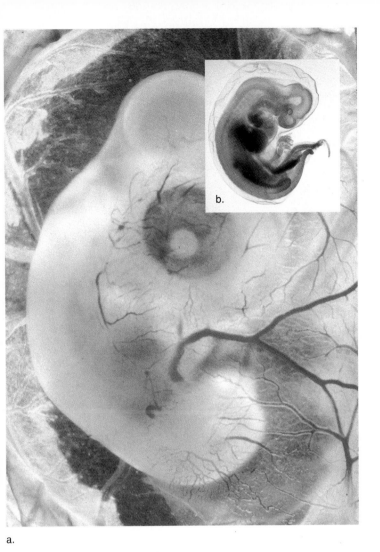

Chick Embryo vs. Pig Embryo
Figure 19.16

Stabilizing Selection
Figure 20.6

initial
distribution

birth
weight

after
time

after
more
time

Stabilizing Selection

Key

Number of Individuals

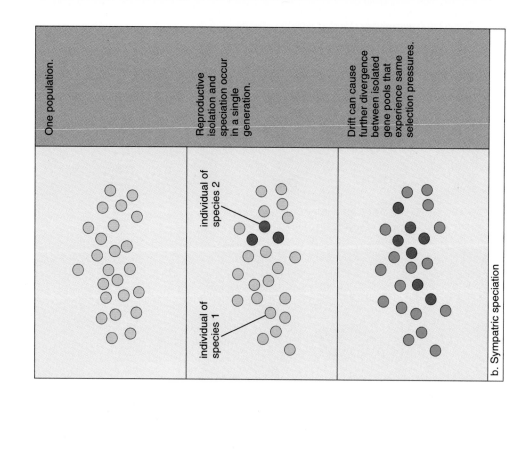

Allopatric Speciation
Figure 20.11a

a. Allopatric speciation

Two populations experience gene flow.

Gene flow is interrupted by geographic barrier. Variant types appear.

Drift and selection cause divergence between isolated gene pools.

Reproductive isolation is present even though geographic barrier has been removed. Speciation is complete.

population 1

population 2

gene flow

geographic barrier

variant type

variant type

geographic barrier

individual of species 2

individual of species 1

Sympatric Speciation
Figure 20.11b

b. Sympatric speciation

One population.

Reproductive isolation and speciation occur in a single generation.

Drift can cause further divergence between isolated gene pools that experience same selection pressures.

individual of species 2

individual of species 1

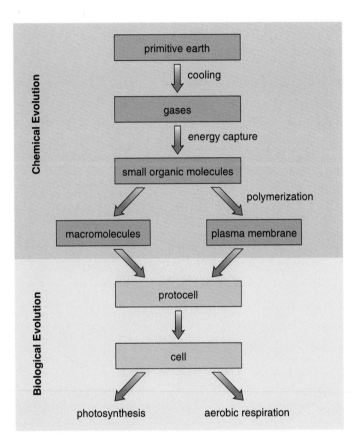

Chemical Evolution Diagram
Figure 21.4

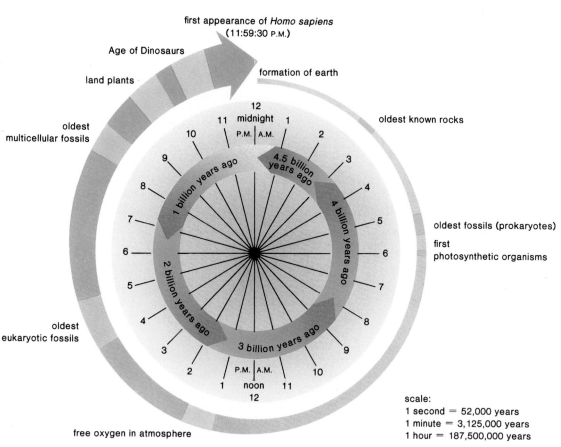

History of Earth Using a 24-hour Time Scale
Figure 21.5

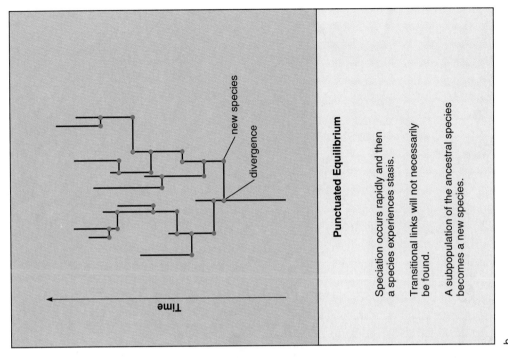

Phyletic Gradualism

Speciation occurs gradually and stasis is apparent rather than real.

Transitional links should be found.

An ancestral species can be transformed into a new species.

a.

Punctuated Equilibrium

Speciation occurs rapidly and then a species experiences stasis.

Transitional links will not necessarily be found.

A subpopulation of the ancestral species becomes a new species.

b.

Phyletic & Punctuated Gradualism Diagrams
Figure 21.18

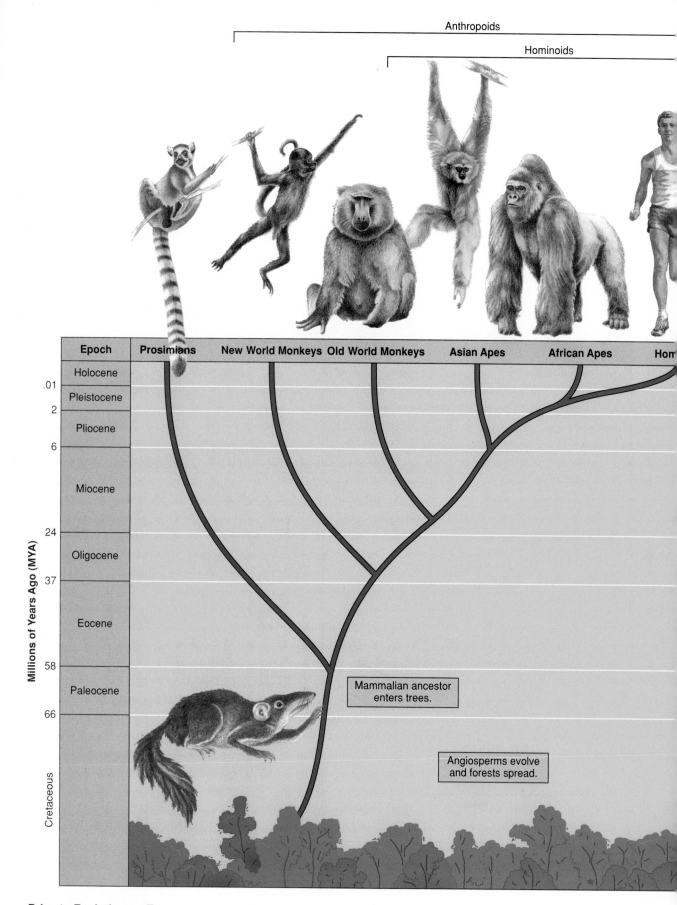

Primate Evolutionary Tree
Figure 22.3

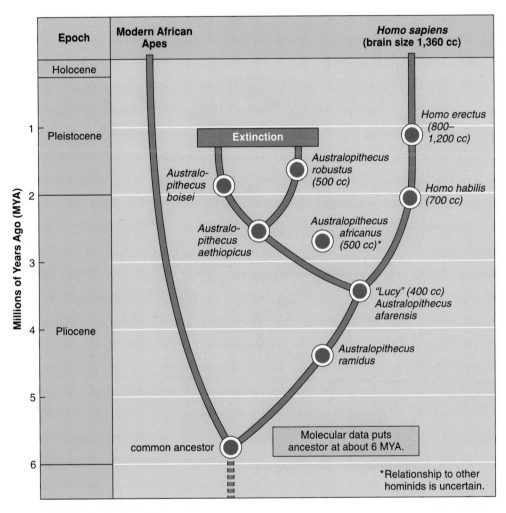

Hominoid Evolutionary Tree
Figure 22.9

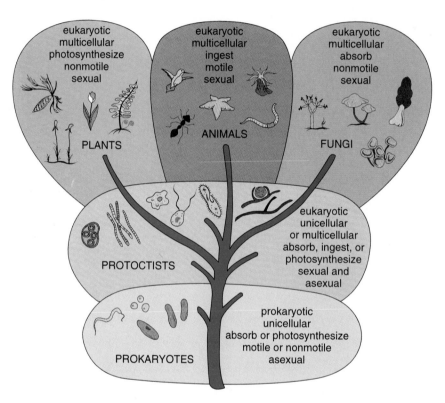

eukaryotic
multicellular
photosynthesize
nonmotile
sexual

PLANTS

eukaryotic
multicellular
ingest
motile
sexual

ANIMALS

eukaryotic
multicellular
absorb
nonmotile
sexual

FUNGI

eukaryotic
unicellular
or multicellular
absorb, ingest, or
photosynthesize
sexual and
asexual

PROTOCTISTS

prokaryotic
unicellular
absorb or photosynthesize
motile or nonmotile
asexual

PROKARYOTES

Five-Kingdom System of Classification
Figure 23.6

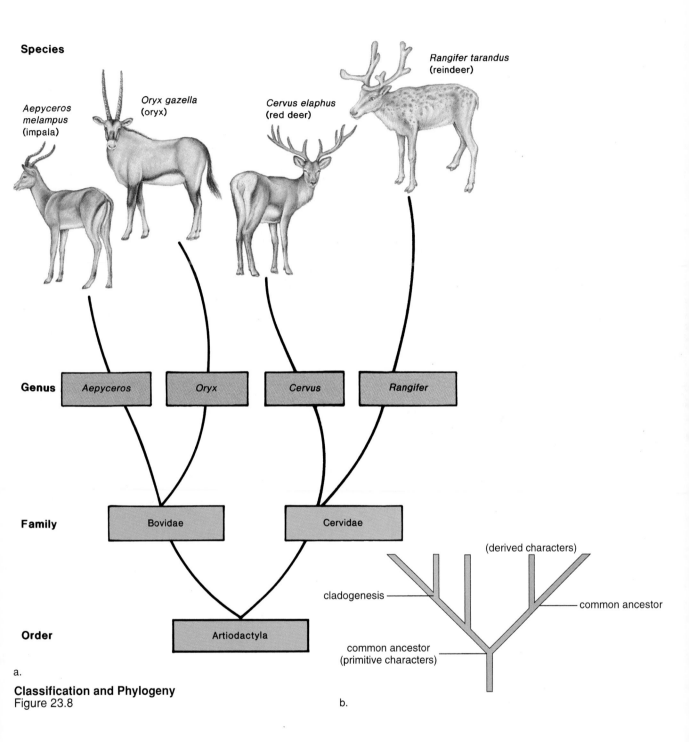

Species

Aepyceros melampus (impala)

Oryx gazella (oryx)

Cervus elaphus (red deer)

Rangifer tarandus (reindeer)

Genus

| *Aepyceros* | *Oryx* | *Cervus* | *Rangifer* |

Family

| Bovidae | Cervidae |

Order

| Artiodactyla |

a.

(derived characters)

cladogenesis

common ancestor

common ancestor (primitive characters)

b.

Classification and Phylogeny
Figure 23.8

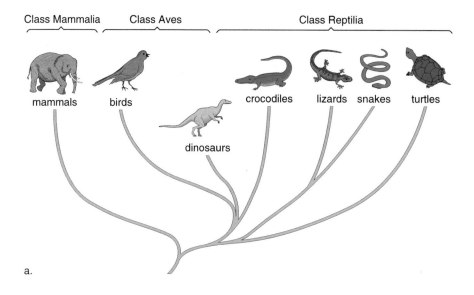

a.

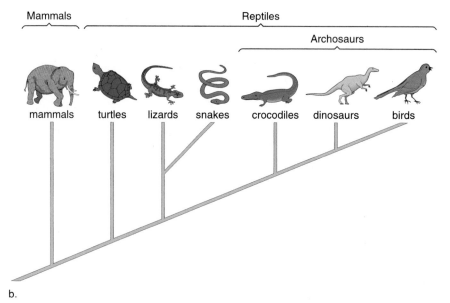

b.

Traditional vs. Cladistic View of Phylogeny
Figure 23.11

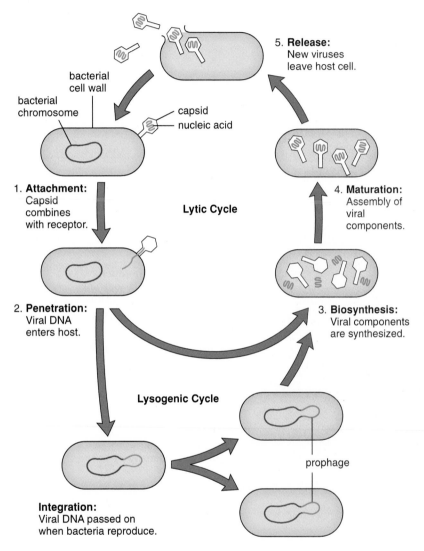

5. **Release:**
   New viruses
   leave host cell.

bacterial
cell wall

bacterial
chromosome

capsid
nucleic acid

Lytic Cycle

1. **Attachment:**
   Capsid
   combines
   with receptor.

4. **Maturation:**
   Assembly of
   viral
   components.

2. **Penetration:**
   Viral DNA
   enters host.

3. **Biosynthesis:**
   Viral components
   are synthesized.

Lysogenic Cycle

prophage

Integration:
Viral DNA passed on
when bacteria reproduce.

Lytic vs. Lysogenic Cycles
Figure 24.3

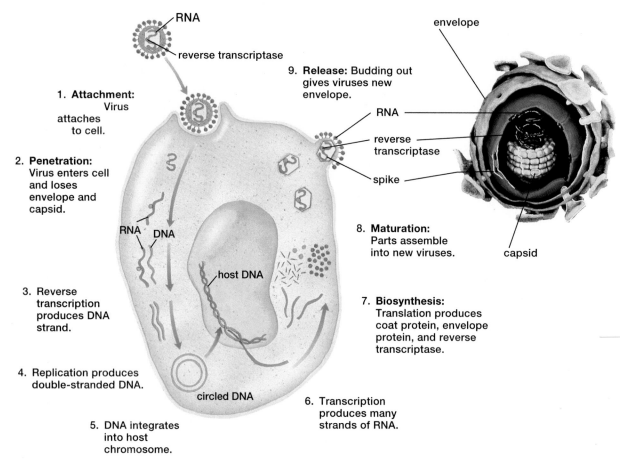

RNA

reverse transcriptase

envelope

9. **Release:** Budding out gives viruses new envelope.

RNA

1. **Attachment:** Virus attaches to cell.

reverse transcriptase

spike

2. **Penetration:** Virus enters cell and loses envelope and capsid.

RNA   DNA

host DNA

8. **Maturation:** Parts assemble into new viruses.

capsid

3. Reverse transcription produces DNA strand.

7. **Biosynthesis:** Translation produces coat protein, envelope protein, and reverse transcriptase.

4. Replication produces double-stranded DNA.

circled DNA

6. Transcription produces many strands of RNA.

5. DNA integrates into host chromosome.

Reproduction of a Retrovirus
Figure 24.4

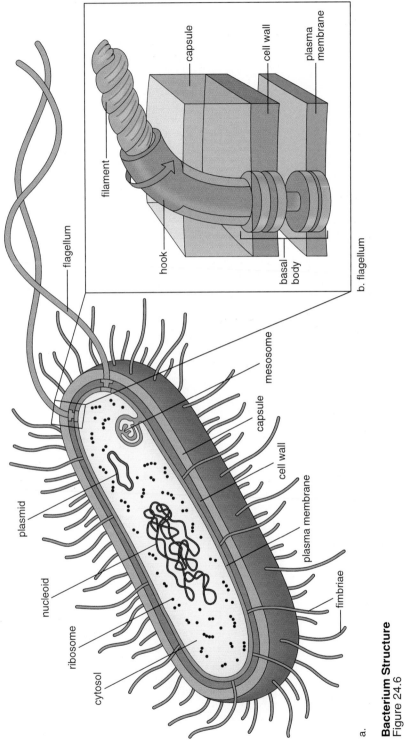

Bacterium Structure
Figure 24.6

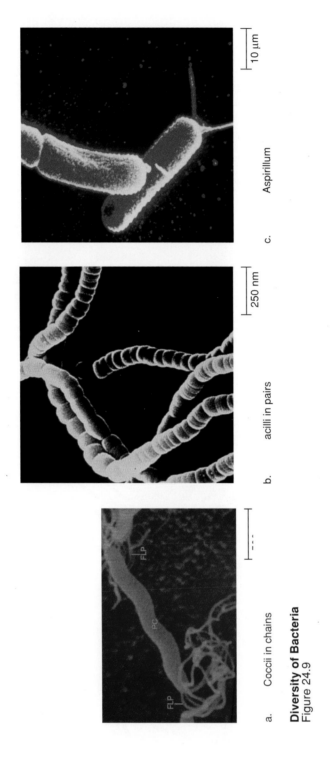

c. Aspirillum

⊢ 10 μm

b. acilli in pairs

⊢ 250 nm

a. Coccii in chains

Diversity of Bacteria
Figure 24.9

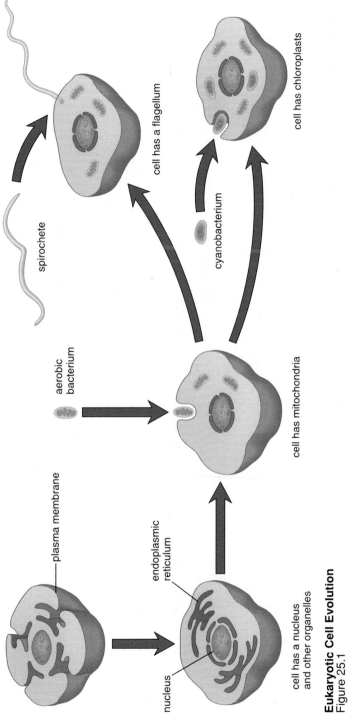

Eukaryotic Cell Evolution
Figure 25.1

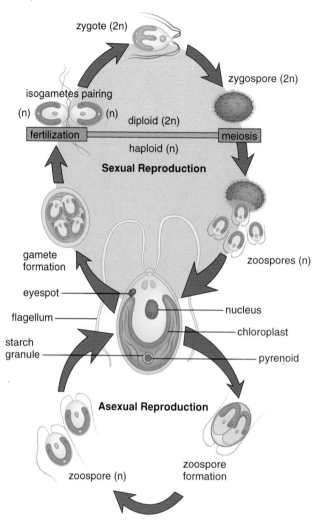

zygote (2n)

zygospore (2n)

isogametes pairing

(n)   (n)   diploid (2n)

fertilization   meiosis

haploid (n)

Sexual Reproduction

zoospores (n)

gamete
formation

eyespot

nucleus

flagellum

chloroplast

starch
granule

pyrenoid

Asexual Reproduction

zoospore (n)

zoospore
formation

Structure and Life Cycle of *Chlamydomonas*
Figure 25.2

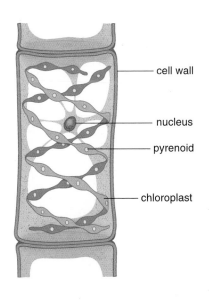

cell wall

nucleus

pyrenoid

chloroplast

Spirogyra **Anatomy**
Figure 25.4

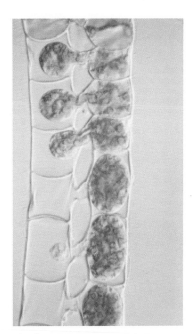

20 µm

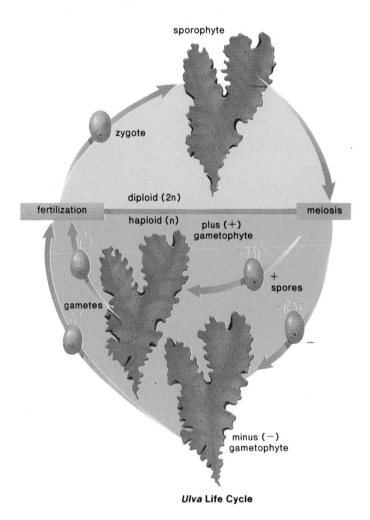

sporophyte

zygote

diploid (2n)

fertilization   meiosis

haploid (n)

plus (+)
gametophyte

+
spores

gametes

−

minus (−)
gametophyte

Ulva **Life Cycle**

Ulva **Life Cycle**
Figure 25.5

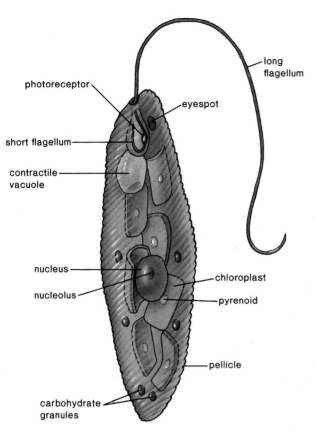

photoreceptor

eyespot

long flagellum

short flagellum

contractile vacuole

nucleus

nucleolus

chloroplast

pyrenoid

pellicle

carbohydrate granules

Euglena **Anatomy**
Figure 25.8

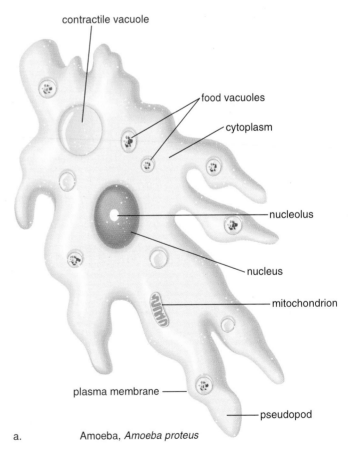

contractile vacuole

food vacuoles

cytoplasm

nucleolus

nucleus

mitochondrion

plasma membrane

pseudopod

a.　　　Amoeba, *Amoeba proteus*

Amoeba **Anatomy**
Figure 25.10*a*

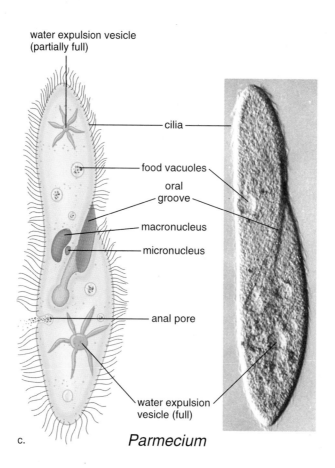

water expulsion vesicle
(partially full)

cilia

food vacuoles

oral
groove

macronucleus

micronucleus

anal pore

water expulsion
vesicle (full)

c.   *Parmecium*

Paramecium Anatomy
Figure 25.11*c*

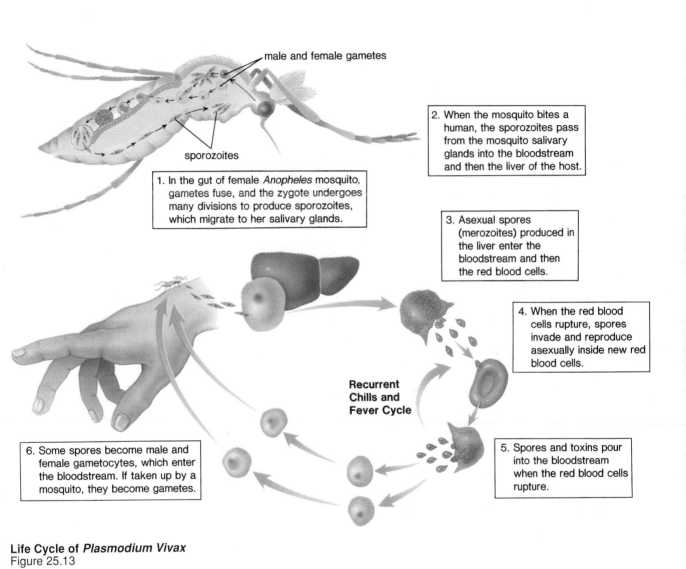

male and female gametes

sporozoites

1. In the gut of female *Anopheles* mosquito, gametes fuse, and the zygote undergoes many divisions to produce sporozoites, which migrate to her salivary glands.

2. When the mosquito bites a human, the sporozoites pass from the mosquito salivary glands into the bloodstream and then the liver of the host.

3. Asexual spores (merozoites) produced in the liver enter the bloodstream and then the red blood cells.

4. When the red blood cells rupture, spores invade and reproduce asexually inside new red blood cells.

Recurrent Chills and Fever Cycle

5. Spores and toxins pour into the bloodstream when the red blood cells rupture.

6. Some spores become male and female gametocytes, which enter the bloodstream. If taken up by a mosquito, they become gametes.

Life Cycle of *Plasmodium Vivax*
Figure 25.13

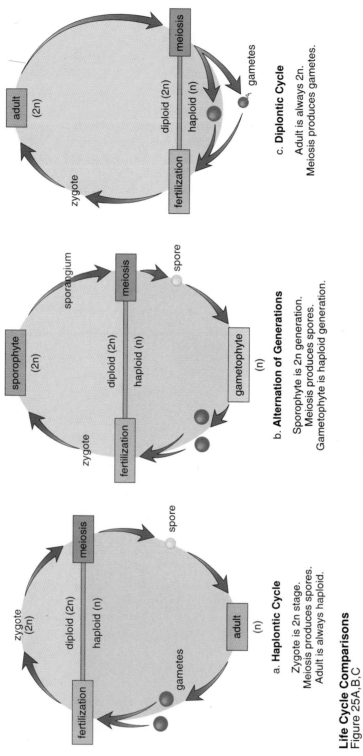

a. Haplontic Cycle

Zygote is 2n stage.
Meiosis produces spores.
Adult is always haploid.

b. Alternation of Generations

Sporophyte is 2n generation.
Meiosis produces spores.
Gametophyte is haploid generation.

c. Diplontic Cycle

Adult is always 2n.
Meiosis produces gametes.

Life Cycle Comparisons
Figure 25A,B,C

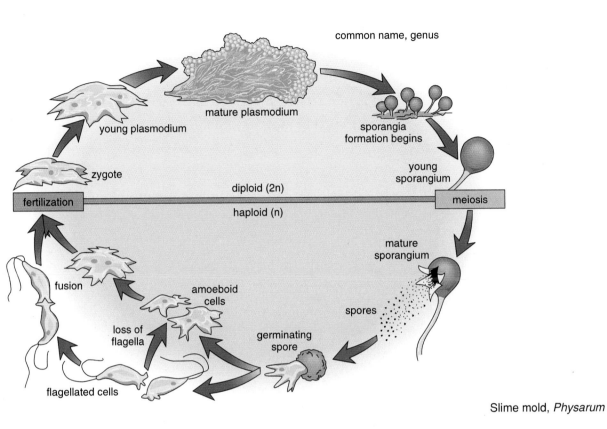

common name, genus

mature plasmodium

young plasmodium

sporangia
formation begins

zygote

young
sporangium

diploid (2n)

fertilization

meiosis

haploid (n)

mature
sporangium

fusion

amoeboid
cells

spores

loss of
flagella

germinating
spore

flagellated cells

Slime mold, *Physarum*

1 mm

Slime Mold Life Cycle
Figure 25.14

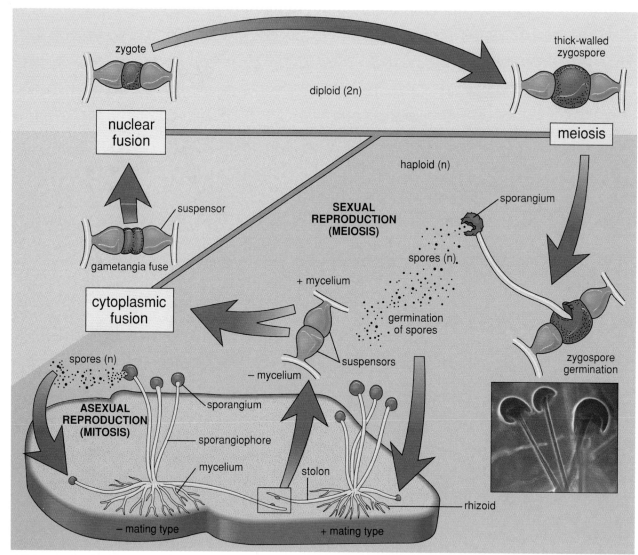

Rhizopus Stolonifer Life Cycle
Figure 26.3

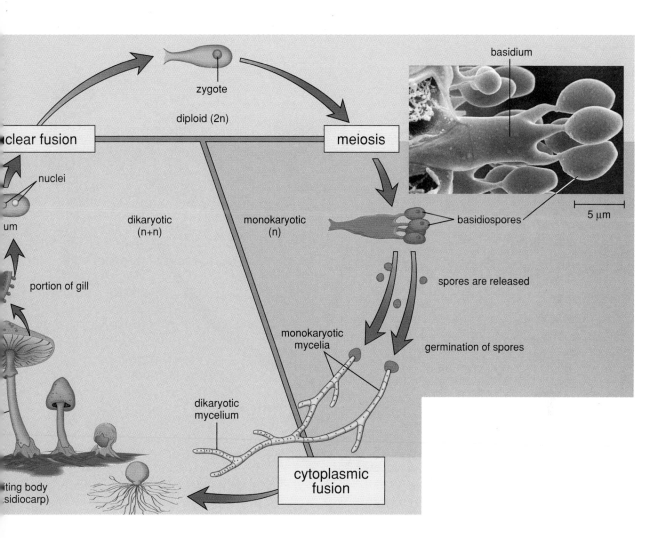

basidium

zygote

diploid (2n)

clear fusion

meiosis

nuclei

dikaryotic
(n+n)

monokaryotic
(n)

5 µm

basidiospores

um

portion of gill

spores are released

monokaryotic
mycelia

germination of spores

dikaryotic
mycelium

cytoplasmic
fusion

iting body
sidiocarp)

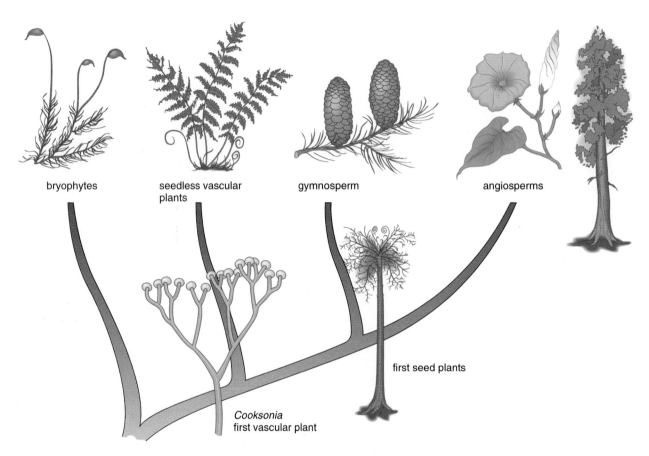

bryophytes

seedless vascular plants

gymnosperm

angiosperms

Cooksonia first vascular plant

first seed plants

Evolution of the Major Groups of Plants
Figure 27.1

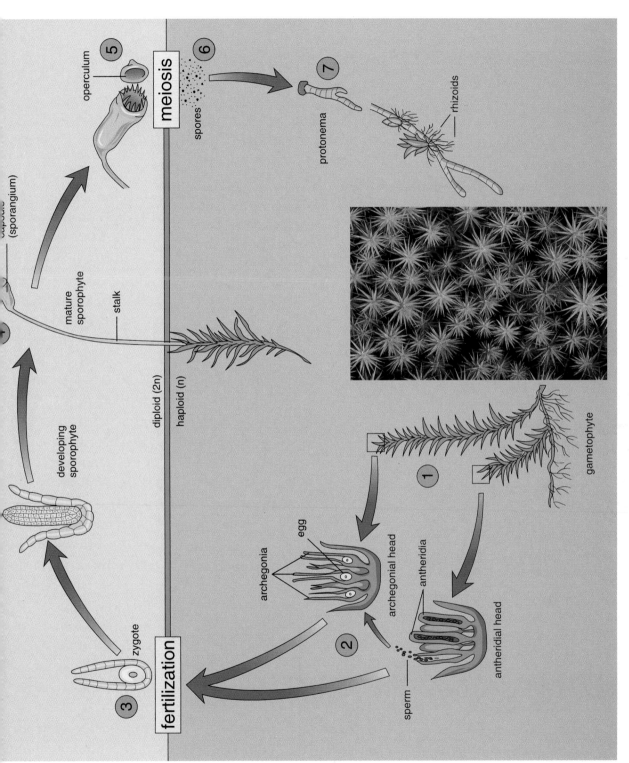

Moss Life Cycle
Figure 27.3

117

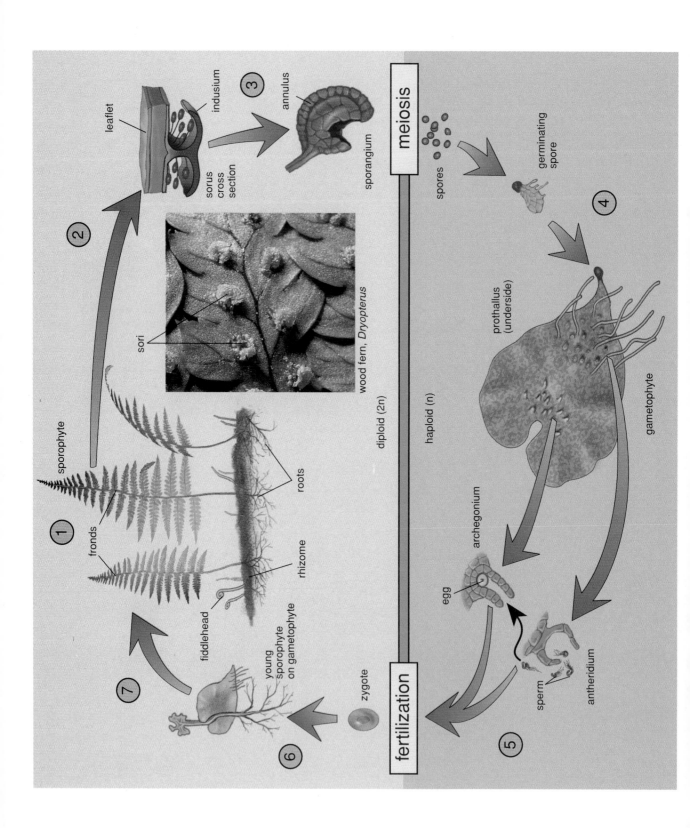

sporophyte

fronds

roots

rhizome

fiddlehead

young sporophyte on gametophyte

leaflet

indusium

sorus cross section

annulus

sporangium

sori

wood fern, *Dryopterus*

diploid (2n)

haploid (n)

meiosis

spores

germinating spore

prothallus (underside)

gametophyte

archegonium

egg

antheridium

sperm

fertilization

zygote

① ② ③ ④ ⑤ ⑥ ⑦

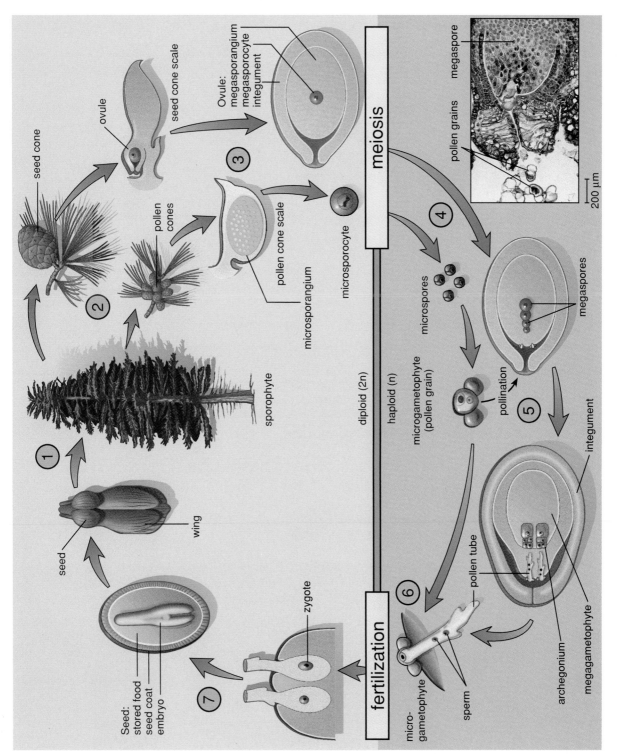

Pine Life Cycle
Figure 27.10

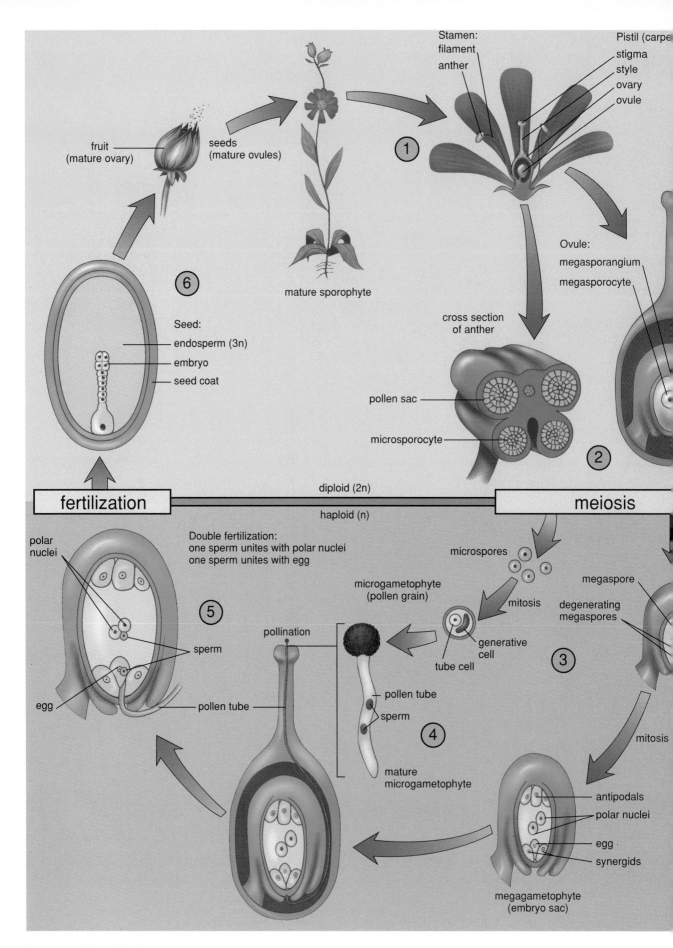

Flowering Plant Life Cycle
Figure 27.13

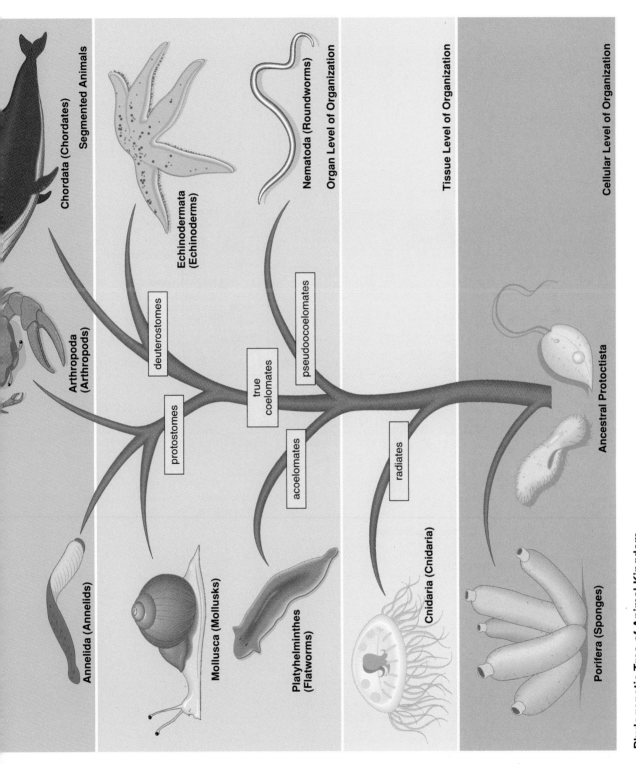

Chordata (Chordates)   Segmented Animals

Echinodermata (Echinoderms)

Nematoda (Roundworms)

Organ Level of Organization

Tissue Level of Organization

Cellular Level of Organization

deuterostomes

protostomes

true coelomates

pseudocoelomates

acoelomates

radiates

Arthropoda (Arthropods)

Annelida (Annelids)

Mollusca (Mollusks)

Platyhelminthes (Flatworms)

Cnidaria (Cnidaria)

Porifera (Sponges)

Ancestral Protoctista

Phylogenetic Tree of Animal Kingdom
Figure 28.2

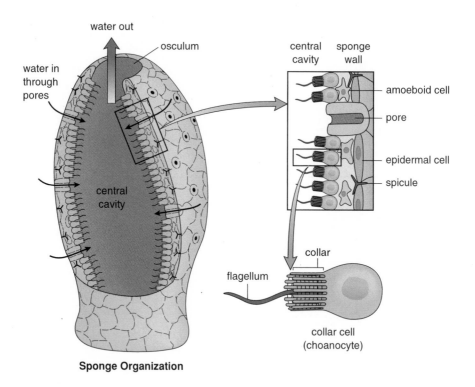

Sponge Organization

Sponge Anatomy
Figure 28.3

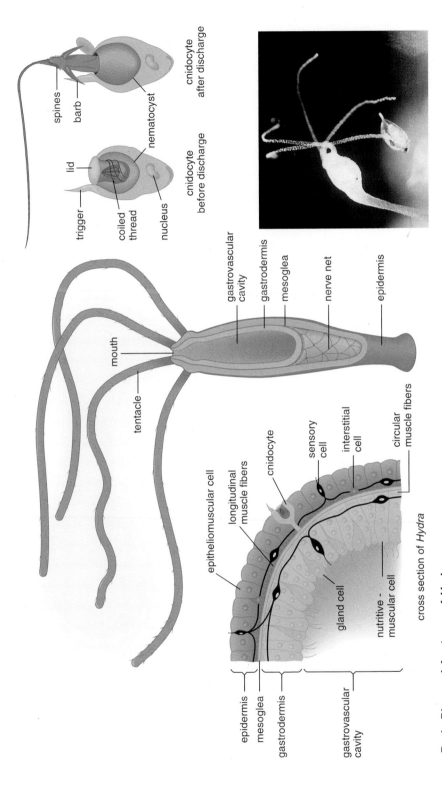

spines

barb

cnidocyte
after discharge

lid

nematocyst

trigger

coiled
thread

nucleus

cnidocyte
before discharge

gastrovascular
cavity

gastrodermis

mesoglea

nerve net

epidermis

mouth

tentacle

epitheliomuscular cell

longitudinal
muscle fibers

cnidocyte

sensory
cell

interstitial
cell

circular
muscle fibers

gland cell

nutritive -
muscular cell

cross section of *Hydra*

epidermis

mesoglea

gastrodermis

gastrovascular
cavity

Body Plan and Anatomy of *Hydra*
Figure 28.6

123

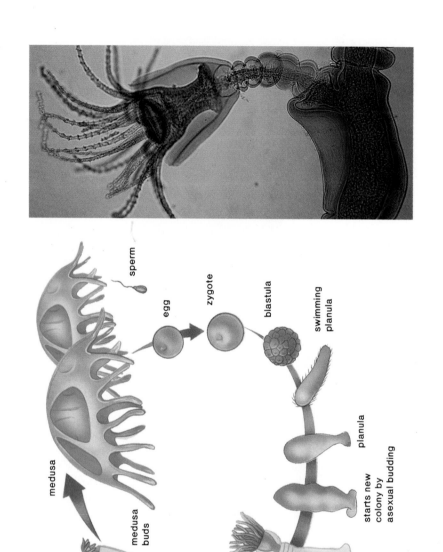

Obelia Structure and Life Cycle
Figure 28.7

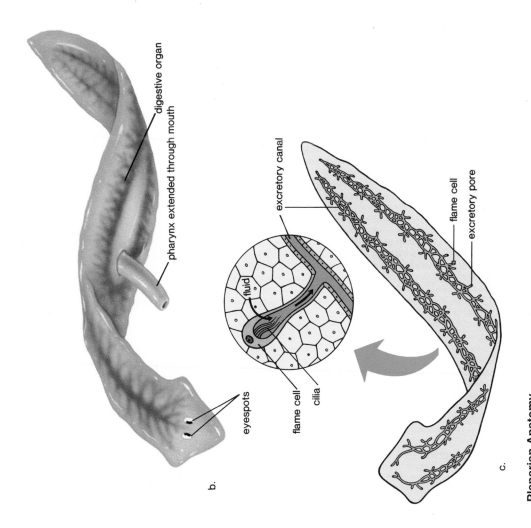

digestive organ

pharynx extended through mouth

eyespots

b.

excretory canal

fluid

flame cell

cilia

flame cell

excretory pore

c.

Planarian Anatomy
Figure 28.9*b,c*

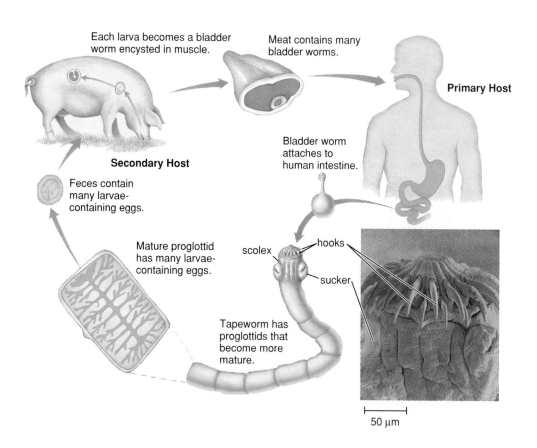

Each larva becomes a bladder worm encysted in muscle.

Meat contains many bladder worms.

Primary Host

Secondary Host

Bladder worm attaches to human intestine.

Feces contain many larvae-containing eggs.

Mature proglottid has many larvae-containing eggs.

scolex

hooks

sucker

Tapeworm has proglottids that become more mature.

50 μm

Life Cycle of a Tapeworm
Figure 28.11

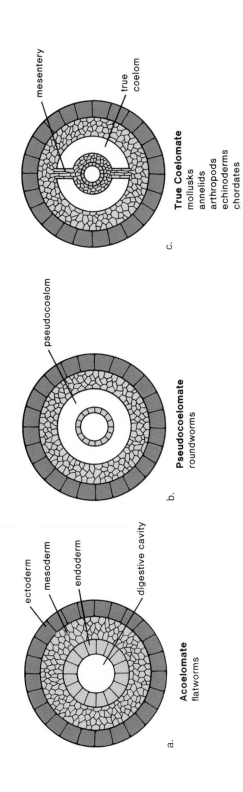

Acoelom, Pseudocoelom, True Coelom Comparison
Figure 28A

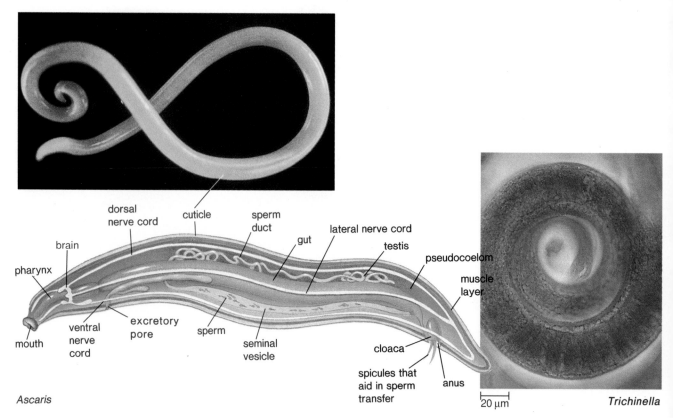

Ascaris

Trichinella

20 μm

Roundworm Anatomy
Figure 28.12

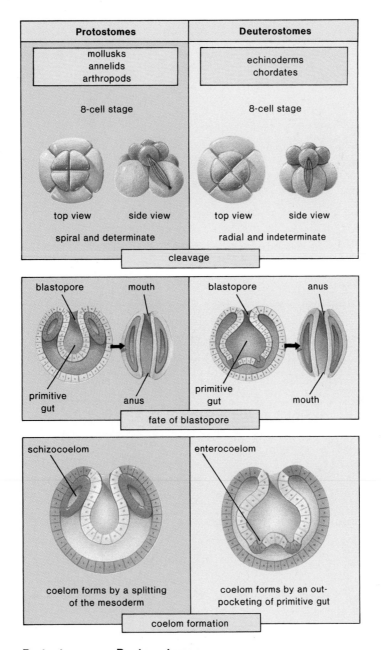

Protostomes vs. Deuterostomes
Figure 29.1

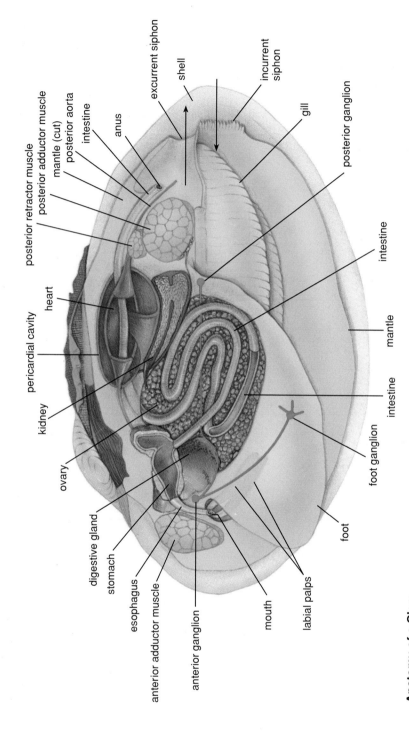

posterior retractor muscle
posterior adductor muscle
mantle (cut)
posterior aorta
intestine
anus
excurrent siphon
shell
incurrent siphon
gill
posterior ganglion
intestine
mantle
intestine
foot ganglion
foot
labial palps
mouth
anterior ganglion
anterior adductor muscle
esophagus
stomach
digestive gland
ovary
kidney
pericardial cavity
heart

Anatomy of a Clam
Figure 29.3

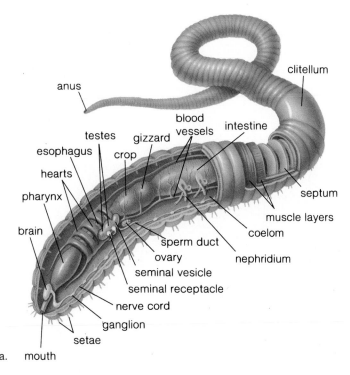

anus

clitellum

blood
vessels

intestine

testes

gizzard

esophagus

crop

hearts

septum

pharynx

muscle layers

brain

coelom

sperm duct

nephridium

ovary

seminal vesicle

seminal receptacle

nerve cord

ganglion

setae

a.　mouth

Earthworm Anatomy
Figure 29.7*a*

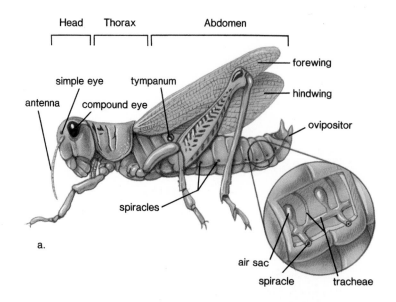

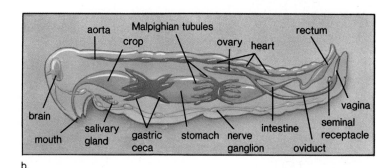

b.

Grasshopper Anatomy
Figure 29.14

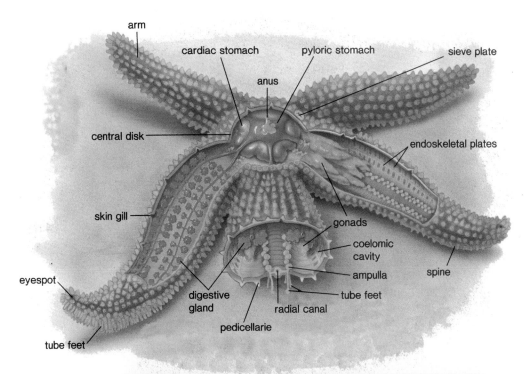

arm

cardiac stomach   pyloric stomach   sieve plate

anus

central disk   endoskeletal plates

skin gill   gonads

coelomic
cavity

ampulla

eyespot   spine

digestive   tube feet
gland   radial canal

pedicellarie

tube feet

a.

Red sea star, *Oreaster*

Seastar Anatomy
Figure 30.1*a*

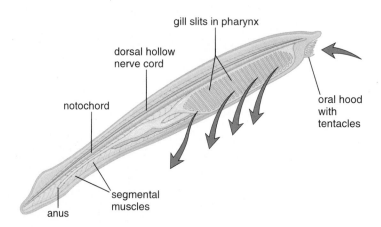

gill slits in pharynx

dorsal hollow
nerve cord

notochord

oral hood
with
tentacles

anus

segmental
muscles

Lancelet Anatomy
Figure 30.4

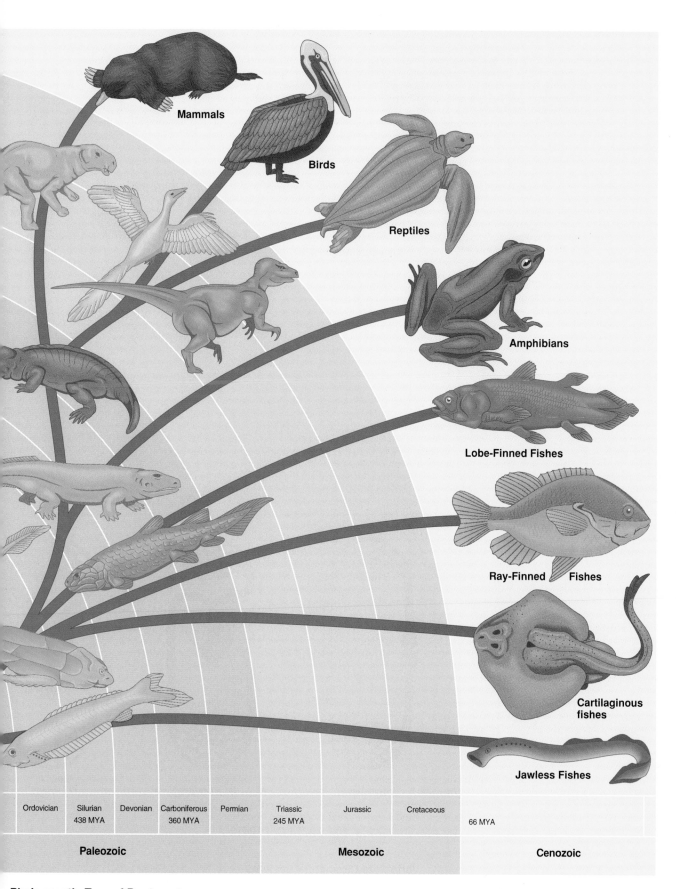

Ordovician	Silurian 438 MYA	Devonian	Carboniferous 360 MYA	Permian	Triassic 245 MYA	Jurassic	Cretaceous	66 MYA
Paleozoic					Mesozoic			Cenozoic

Phylogenetic Tree of Deuterostomes
Figure 30.5

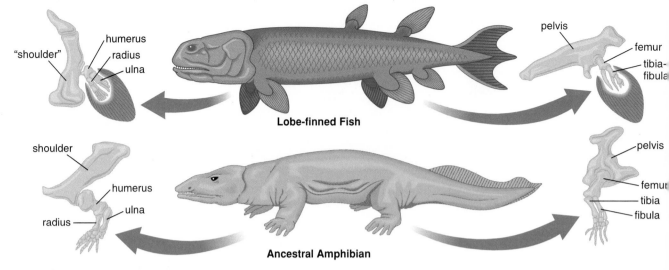

Primitive Amphibian/Lobe-Finned Fish Comparison
Figure 30.9

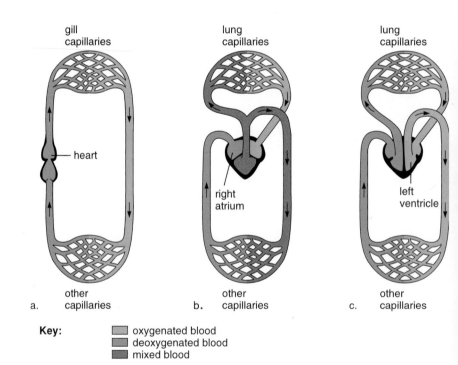

Key:
oxygenated blood
deoxygenated blood
mixed blood

Vertebrate Circulatory Systems
Figure 30.10

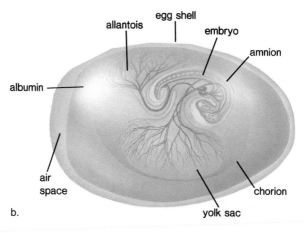

allantois
egg shell
embryo
amnion
albumin
air
space
chorion
yolk sac
b.

Reptilian Egg
Figure 30.12*b*

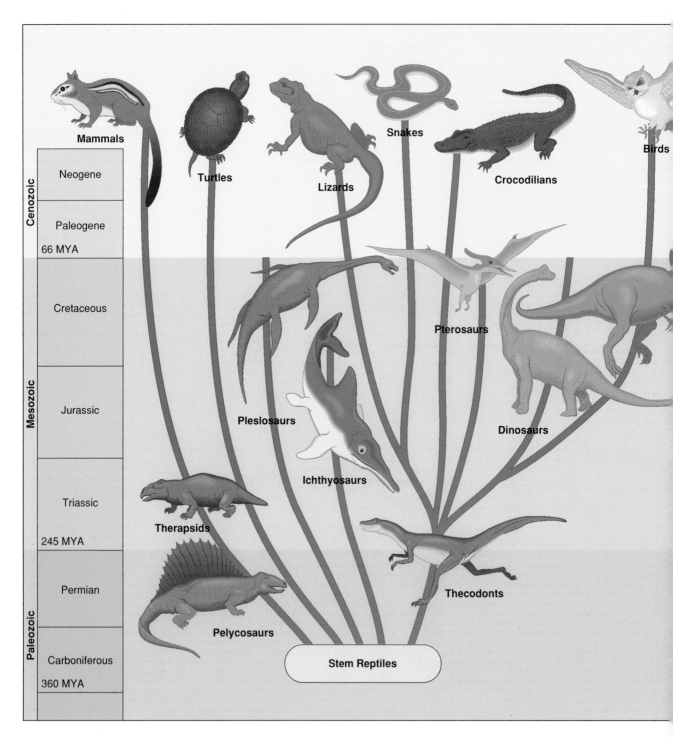

Phylogenetic Tree of Reptiles, Birds, Mammals
Figure 30.13

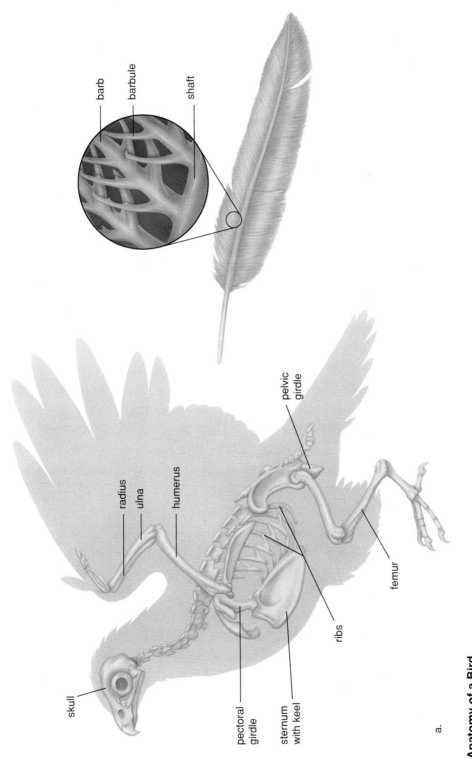

barb
barbule
shaft

pelvic girdle

radius
ulna
humerus

femur

skull

pectoral girdle

sternum with keel

ribs

a.

Anatomy of a Bird
Figure 30.15a

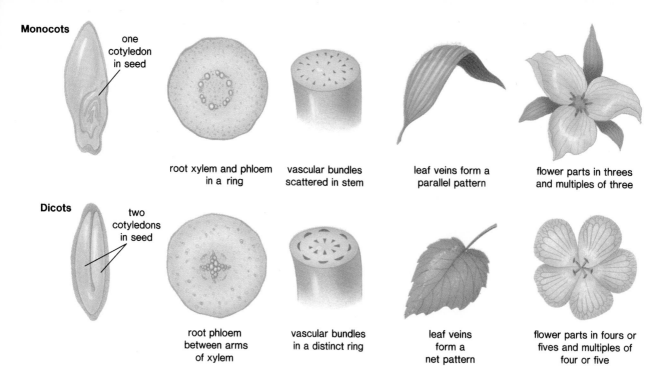

Monocots — one cotyledon in seed

root xylem and phloem in a ring

vascular bundles scattered in stem

leaf veins form a parallel pattern

flower parts in threes and multiples of three

Dicots — two cotyledons in seed

root phloem between arms of xylem

vascular bundles in a distinct ring

leaf veins form a net pattern

flower parts in fours or fives and multiples of four or five

Monocots v. Dicots
Figure 31.3

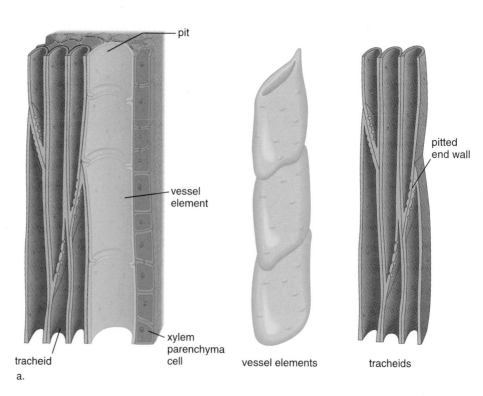

pit

vessel element

xylem parenchyma cell

tracheid

a.

vessel elements

tracheids

pitted end wall

Xylem Structure
Figure 31.6*a*

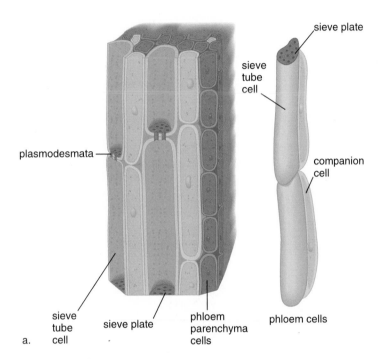

sieve plate

**sieve
tube
cell**

**companion
cell**

plasmodesmata

**sieve
tube
cell**

a.

sieve plate

**phloem
parenchyma
cells**

phloem cells

Phloem Structure
Figure 31.7*a*

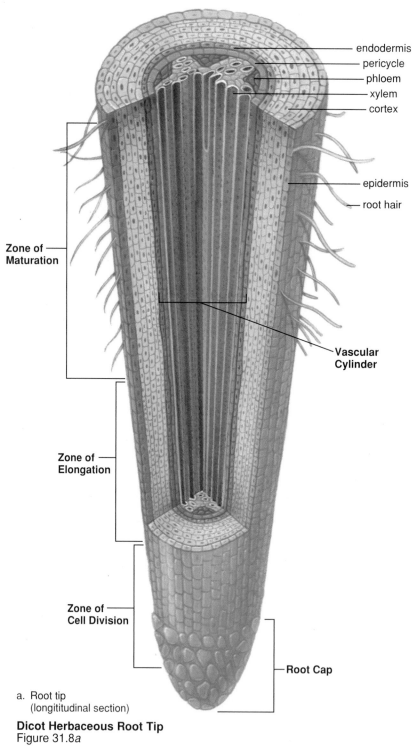

endodermis

pericycle

phloem

xylem

cortex

epidermis

root hair

Zone of Maturation

Vascular Cylinder

Zone of Elongation

Zone of Cell Division

Root Cap

a. Root tip
   (longititudinal section)

Dicot Herbaceous Root Tip
Figure 31.8a

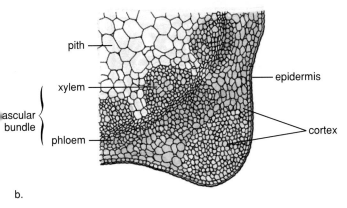

b.

Dicot Stem Anatomy
Figure 31.13*b*

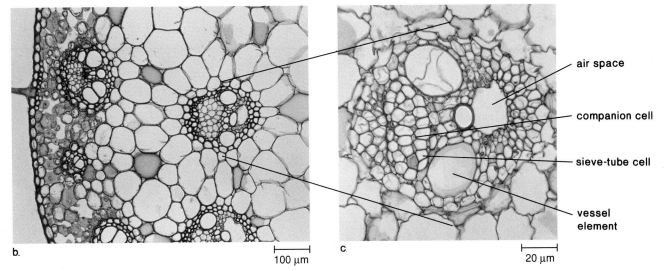

b.   100 μm

c.   20 μm

air space

companion cell

sieve-tube cell

vessel element

Monocot Stem Anatomy
Figure 31.14*b,c*

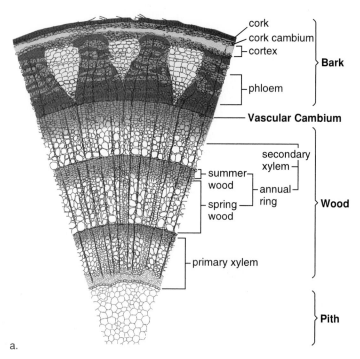

cork
cork cambium
cortex

Bark

phloem

Vascular Cambium

secondary
xylem

summer
wood

annual
ring

spring
wood

Wood

primary xylem

Pith

a.

Dicot Woody Stem
Figure 31.15*a*

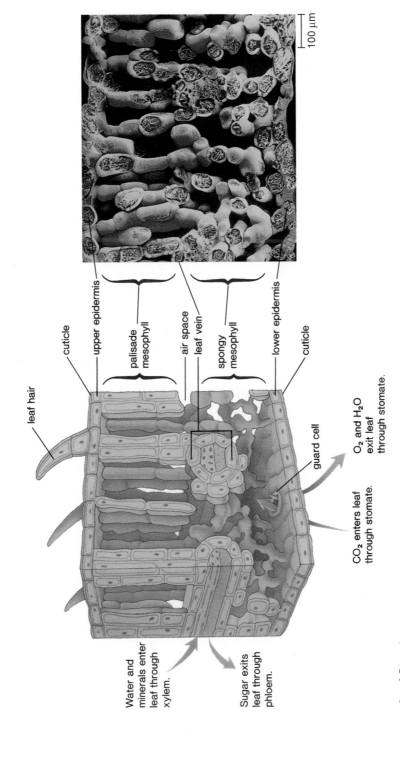

100 μm

leaf hair

cuticle

upper epidermis

palisade mesophyll

air space

leaf vein

spongy mesophyll

lower epidermis

cuticle

guard cell

CO₂ enters leaf through stomate.

O₂ and H₂O exit leaf through stomate.

Water and minerals enter leaf through xylem.

Sugar exits leaf through phloem.

Leaf Structure
Figure 31.18

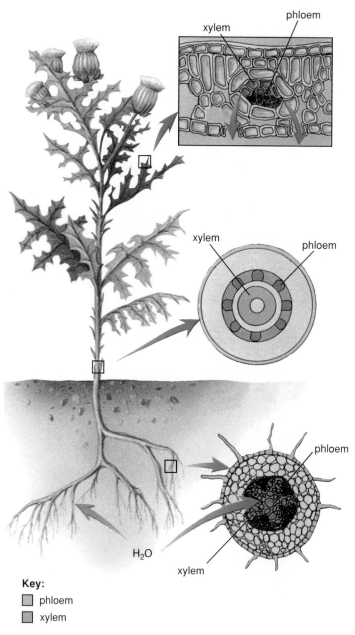

Plants Transport System
Figure 32.1

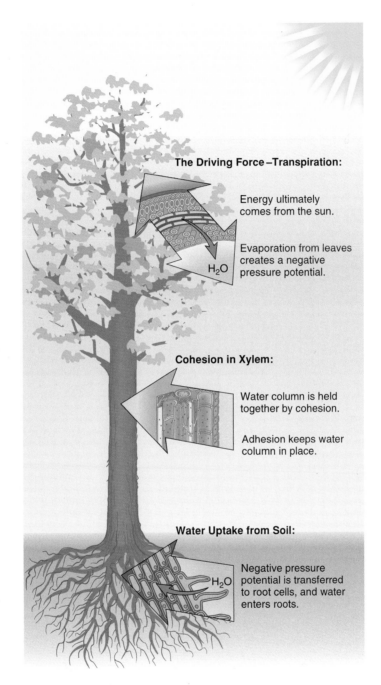

The Driving Force–Transpiration:

Energy ultimately comes from the sun.

H_2O

Evaporation from leaves creates a negative pressure potential.

Cohesion in Xylem:

Water column is held together by cohesion.

Adhesion keeps water column in place.

Water Uptake from Soil:

H_2O

Negative pressure potential is transferred to root cells, and water enters roots.

Cohesion-Tension Model of Xylem Transport
Figure 32.5

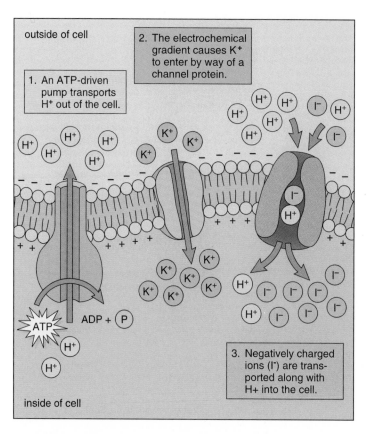

Transport of Minerals Across Plasma Membrane
Figure 32.8

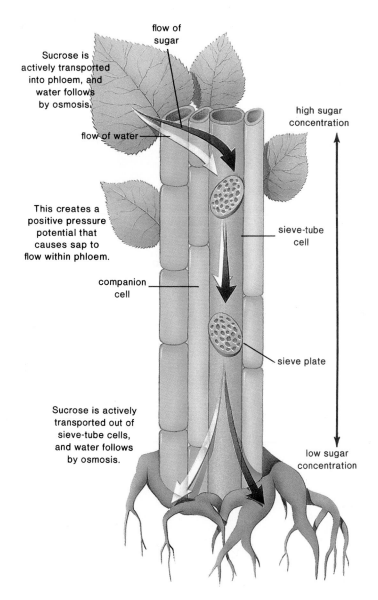

Pressure-Flow Model of Phloem Transport
Figure 32.12

The following text labels appear on the figure:

flow of
sugar

Sucrose is
actively transported
into phloem, and
water follows
by osmosis.

high sugar
concentration

flow of water

This creates a
positive pressure
potential that
causes sap to
flow within phloem.

sieve-tube
cell

companion
cell

sieve plate

Sucrose is actively
transported out of
sieve-tube cells,
and water follows
by osmosis.

low sugar
concentration

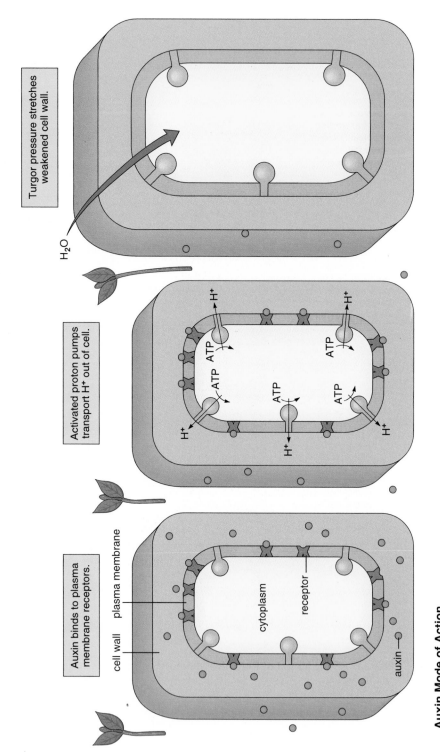

Auxin Mode of Action
Figure 33.8

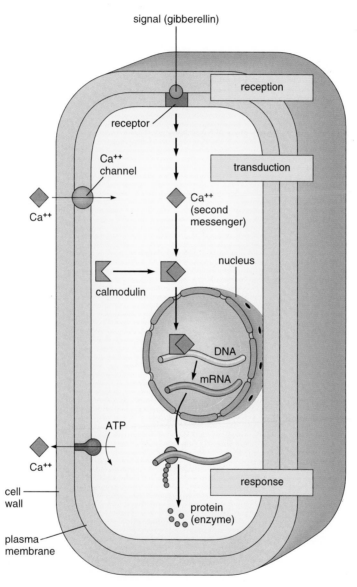

signal (gibberellin)

reception

receptor

Ca++
channel

transduction

Ca++

Ca++
(second
messenger)

nucleus

calmodulin

DNA

mRNA

ATP

Ca++

response

cell
wall

protein
(enzyme)

plasma
membrane

Gibberellin Mode of Action
Figure 33.10

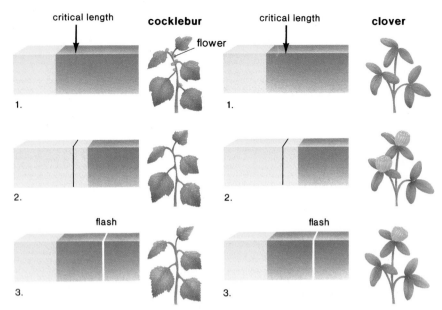

a. Short-Day (Long-Night) Plant

b. Long-Day (Short-Night) Plant

Photoperiodism
Figure 33.14

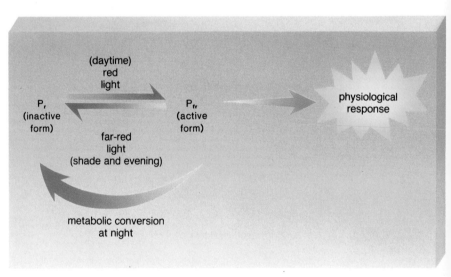

Phytochrome Conversion Cycle
Figure 33.15

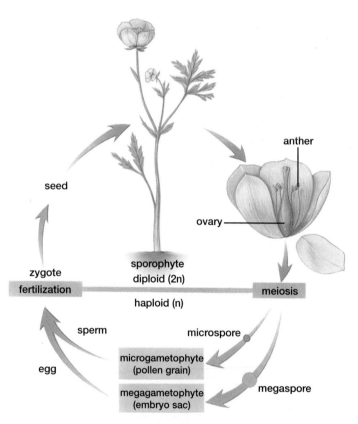

anther

seed

ovary

zygote

sporophyte
diploid (2n)

fertilization

meiosis

haploid (n)

sperm

microspore

microgametophyte
(pollen grain)

egg

megagametophyte
(embryo sac)

megaspore

Alternation of Generations in Flowering Plant
Figure 34.1

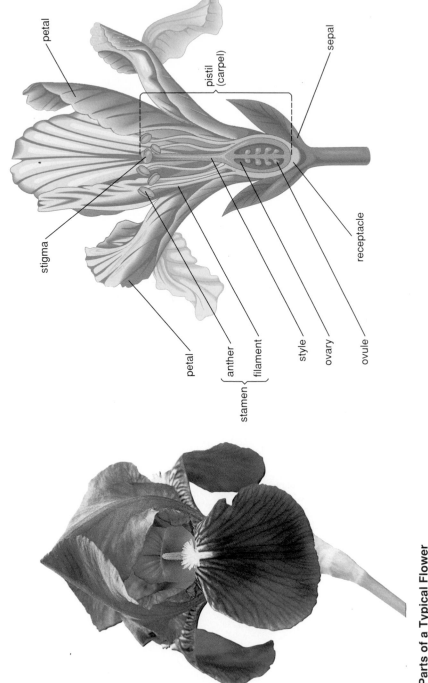

Parts of a Typical Flower
Figure 34.2

petal

pistil
(carpel)

sepal

stigma

petal

anther

stamen

filament

style

ovary

ovule

receptacle

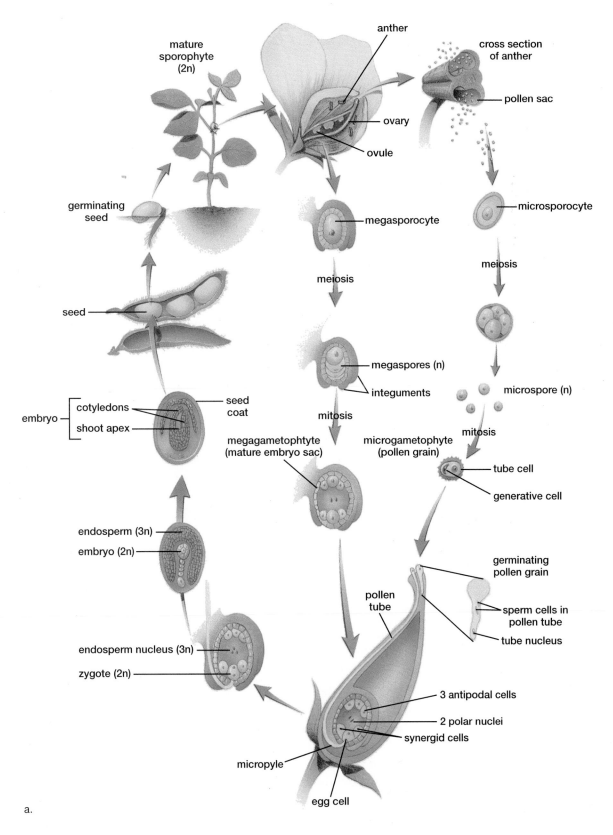

anther

cross section of anther

pollen sac

ovary

ovule

mature sporophyte (2n)

microsporocyte

germinating seed

megasporocyte

meiosis

meiosis

megaspores (n)

microspore (n)

seed

integuments

mitosis

mitosis

embryo

cotyledons

shoot apex

seed coat

megagametophtyte (mature embryo sac)

microgametophyte (pollen grain)

tube cell

generative cell

germinating pollen grain

endosperm (3n)

embryo (2n)

pollen tube

sperm cells in pollen tube

tube nucleus

endosperm nucleus (3n)

zygote (2n)

3 antipodal cells

2 polar nuclei

synergid cells

micropyle

egg cell

a.

Life Cycle of Flowering Plant Diagram
Figure 34.3a

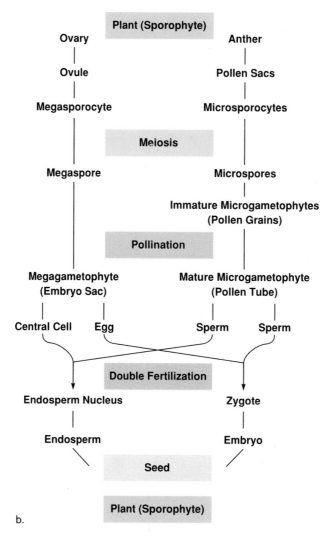

Life Cycle of Flowering Plant Flow Chart
Figure 34.3*b*

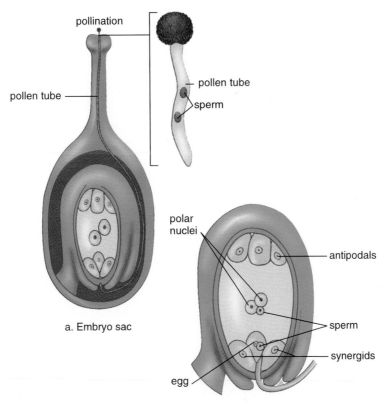

a. Embryo sac

b. Double fertilization

Fertilization
Figure 34.5

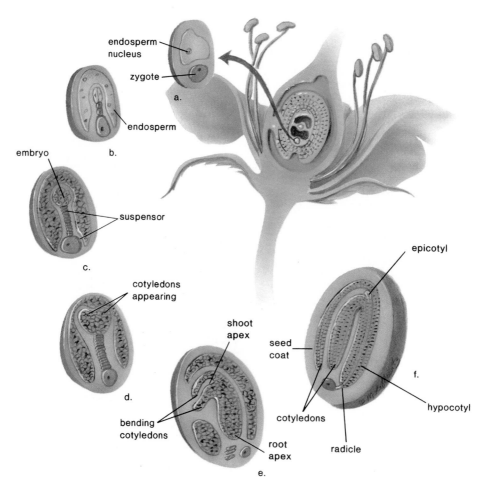

Dicot Embryo Development
Figure 34.6

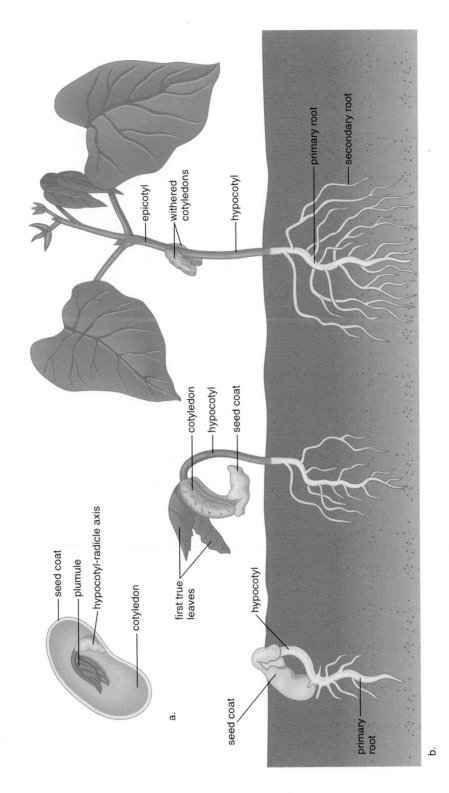

Dicot (bean) Seed Structure and Seedling Development
Figure 34.8

159

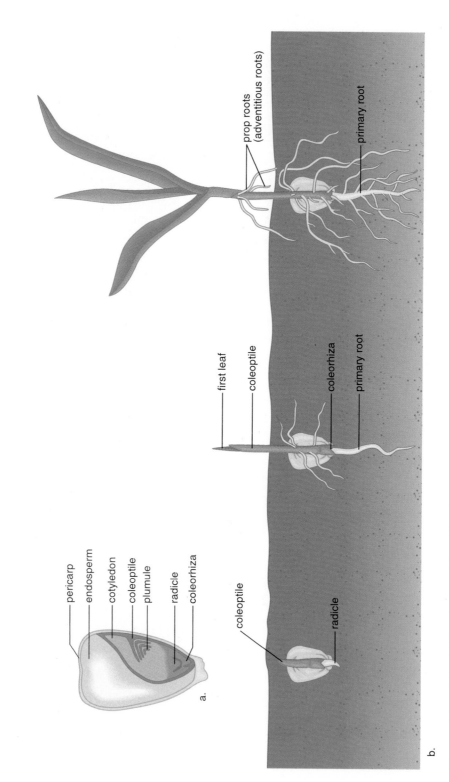

Monocot (corn) Grain Structure and Seedling Development
Figure 34.9

a.

pericarp
endosperm
cotyledon
coleoptile
plumule
radicle
coleorhiza

b.

first leaf
coleoptile
coleorhiza
primary root

coleoptile
radicle

prop roots (adventitious roots)
primary root

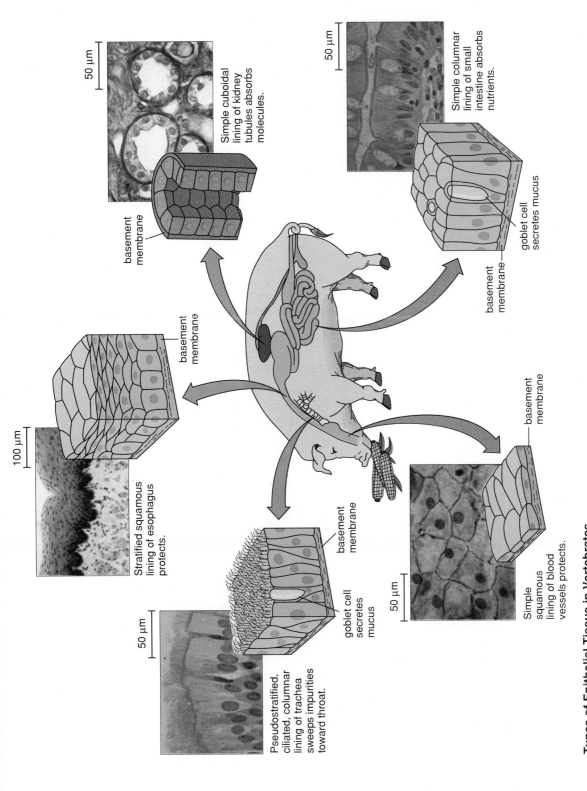

Types of Epithelial Tissue in Vertebrates
Figure 35.2

Simple cuboidal lining of kidney tubules absorbs molecules.

50 μm

basement membrane

Simple columnar lining of small intestine absorbs nutrients.

50 μm

goblet cell secretes mucus

basement membrane

Stratified squamous lining of esophagus protects.

basement membrane

100 μm

Pseudostratified, ciliated, columnar lining of trachea sweeps impurities toward throat.

basement membrane

goblet cell secretes mucus

50 μm

Simple squamous lining of blood vessels protects.

basement membrane

50 μm

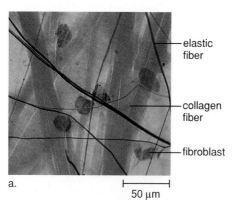

Loose Connective Tissue
has space between components.

Located:
under skin and most epithelial layers

Function:
supports and binds organs

elastic fiber

collagen fiber

fibroblast

a.

50 μm

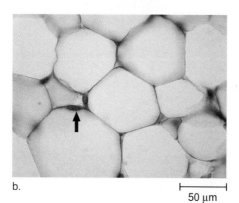

Adipose Tissue
cells are filled with fat.

Located:
under skin, around organs

Function:
insulates, stores fat

b.

50 μm

Hyaline Cartilage
has cells in a lacuna.

Located:
in ends of bones, nose, walls of respiratory passages

Function:
supports, protects

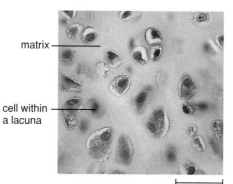

matrix

cell within a lacuna

c.

50 μm

Compact Bone
has cells in concentric rings

Located:
in bones of skeleton

Function:
supports, protects

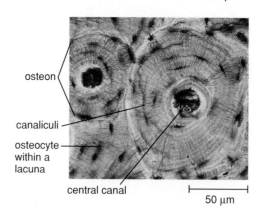

osteon

canaliculi

osteocyte within a lacuna

central canal

d.

50 μm

Examples of Connective Tissue
Figure 35.3

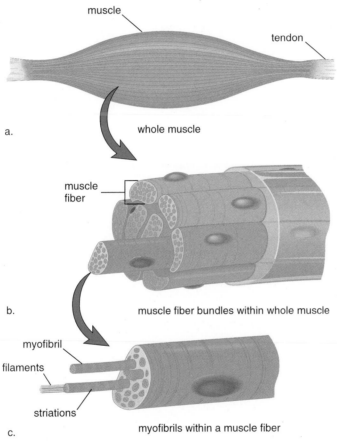

muscle

tendon

a.

whole muscle

muscle
fiber

b.

muscle fiber bundles within whole muscle

myofibril

filaments

striations

c.

myofibrils within a muscle fiber

Components of Whole Muscle
Figure 35.5

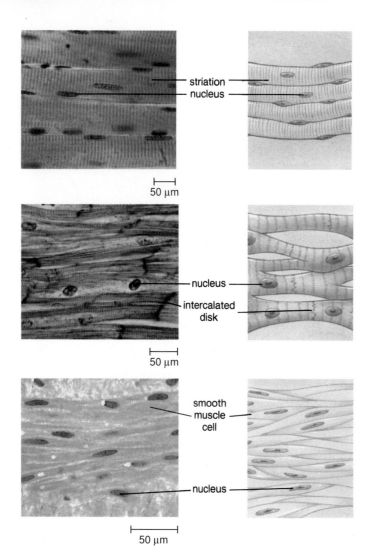

striation

nucleus

50 μm

nucleus

intercalated disk

50 μm

smooth muscle cell

nucleus

50 μm

Muscular Tissue
Figure 35.6

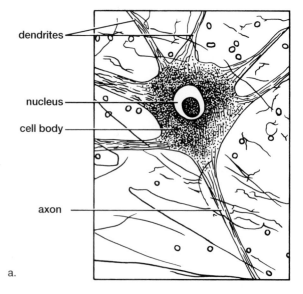

dendrites

nucleus

cell body

axon

a.

Neuron Structure
Figure 35.7a

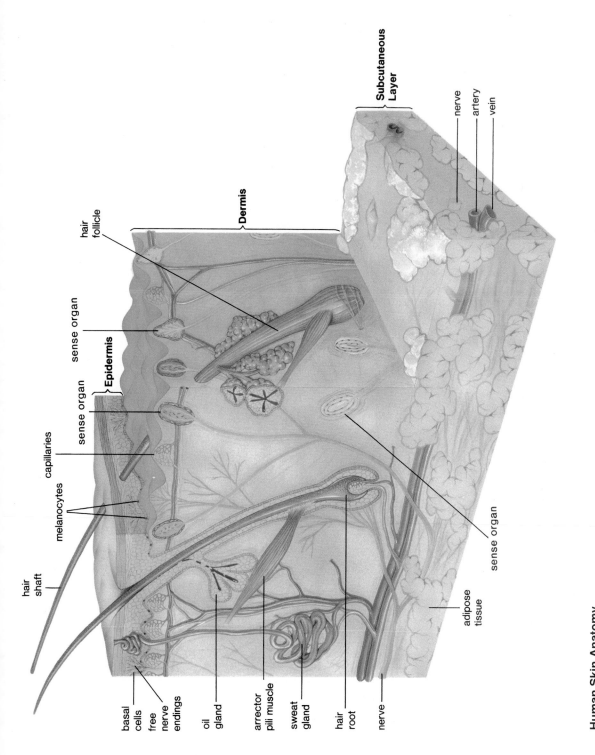

Subcutaneous Layer

nerve

artery

vein

Dermis

hair follicle

sense organ

sense organ

Epidermis

sense organ

capillaries

melanocytes

hair shaft

basal cells

free nerve endings

oil gland

arrector pili muscle

sweat gland

hair root

nerve

sense organ

adipose tissue

Human Skin Anatomy
Figure 35.8

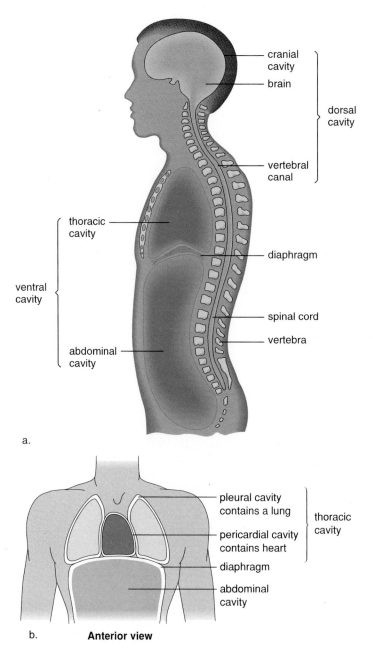

a.

cranial cavity

brain

dorsal cavity

vertebral canal

thoracic cavity

diaphragm

ventral cavity

spinal cord

vertebra

abdominal cavity

b.   **Anterior view**

pleural cavity contains a lung

thoracic cavity

pericardial cavity contains heart

diaphragm

abdominal cavity

Mammalian Body Cavities
Figure 35.9

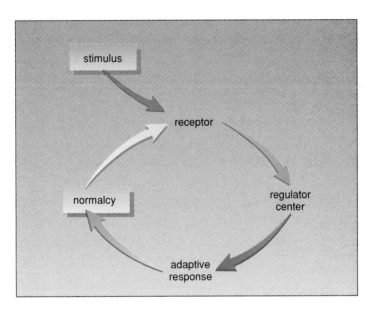

Homeostasis and Negative Feedback Mechanism
Figure 35.10

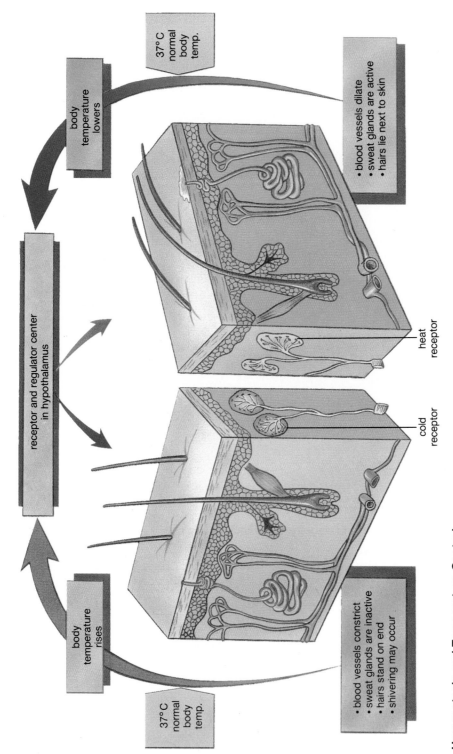

37°C normal body temp.

body temperature lowers

receptor and regulator center in hypothalamus

body temperature rises

37°C normal body temp.

- blood vessels dilate
- sweat glands are active
- hairs lie next to skin

heat receptor

cold receptor

- blood vessels constrict
- sweat glands are inactive
- hairs stand on end
- shivering may occur

Homeostasis and Temperature Control
Figure 35.12

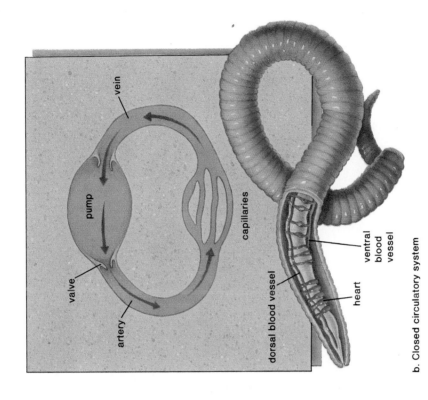

a. Open circulatory system

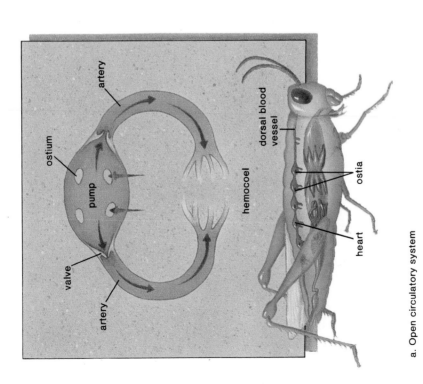

b. Closed circulatory system

Open vs. Closed Circulatory System
Figure 36.2

169

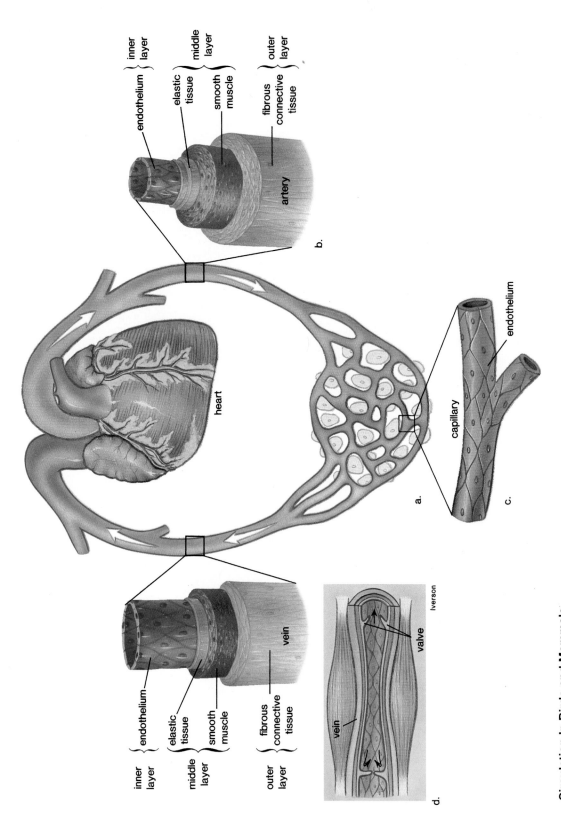

inner layer
{ endothelium

middle layer
{ elastic tissue
smooth muscle

outer layer
{ fibrous connective tissue

artery

b.

endothelium
capillary

c.

heart

a.

endothelium
elastic tissue
smooth muscle
fibrous connective tissue

inner layer
middle layer
outer layer

vein

valve

vein

Iverson

d.

Circulation In Birds and Mammals
Figure 36.3

170

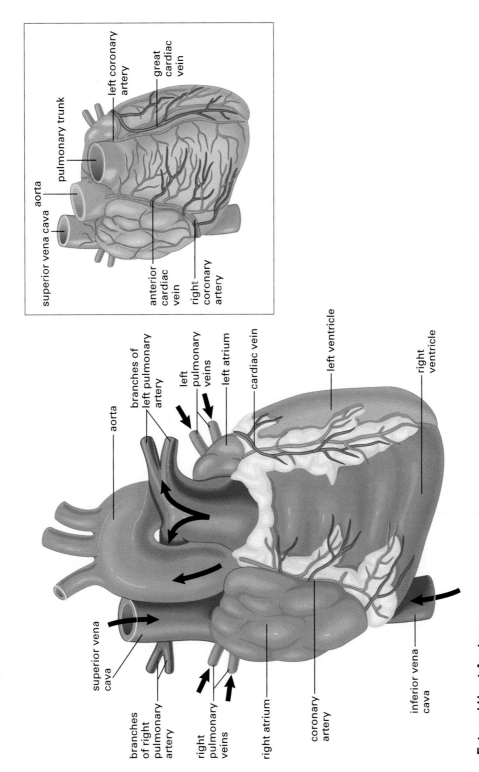

External Heart Anatomy
Figure 36.5

superior vena cava

aorta

pulmonary trunk

left coronary artery

great cardiac vein

anterior cardiac vein

right coronary artery

aorta

branches of left pulmonary artery

left pulmonary veins

left atrium

cardiac vein

left ventricle

right ventricle

superior vena cava

branches of right pulmonary artery

right pulmonary veins

right atrium

coronary artery

inferior vena cava

171

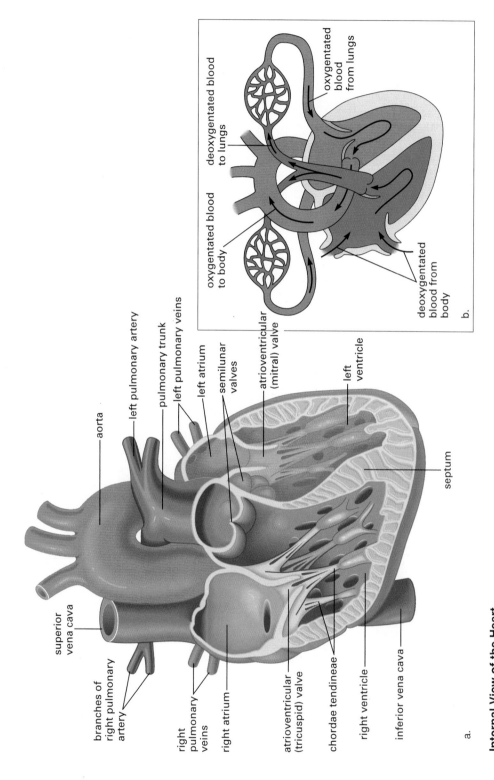

branches of right pulmonary artery

superior vena cava

aorta

left pulmonary artery

pulmonary trunk

left pulmonary veins

left atrium

semilunar valves

atrioventricular (mitral) valve

right pulmonary veins

right atrium

atrioventricular (tricuspid) valve

chordae tendineae

right ventricle

inferior vena cava

left ventricle

septum

a.

deoxygentated blood to lungs

oxygentated blood from lungs

oxygentated blood to body

deoxygentated blood from body

b.

Internal View of the Heart
Figure 36.6

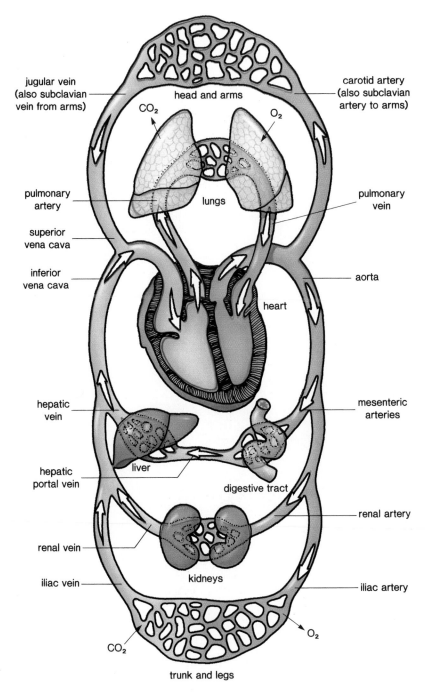

jugular vein
(also subclavian
vein from arms)

head and arms

CO_2

O_2

carotid artery
(also subclavian
artery to arms)

pulmonary
artery

lungs

pulmonary
vein

superior
vena cava

inferior
vena cava

aorta

heart

hepatic
vein

mesenteric
arteries

hepatic
portal vein

liver

digestive tract

renal vein

renal artery

iliac vein

kidneys

iliac artery

CO_2

O_2

trunk and legs

Blood Vessels in the Pulmonary and Systemic Circuits
Figure 36.8

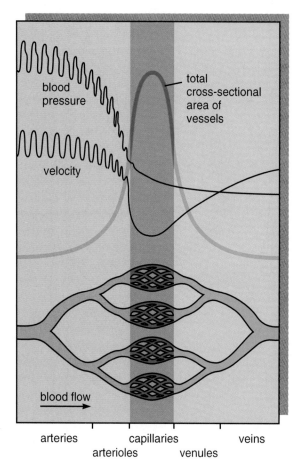

Blood Pressure Diagram
Figure 36.9

Elements	Function and Description	Source
...Blood Cells (...rocytes) ...n–6 million ...³ blood	Transport O_2 and help transport CO_2 7–8 μm in diameter Bright-red to dark-purple biconcave disks without nuclei	Bone marrow
...Blood Cells (...ytes) ...leukocytes* ...sophil ...m³ blood	Fight infection 10–12 μm in diameter Spherical cells with lobed nuclei; large, irregularly shaped, deep-blue granules in cytoplasm	Bone marrow
...sinophil 400 ...m³ blood	10–14 μm in diameter Spherical cells with bilobed nuclei; coarse, deep-red, uniformly sized granules in cytoplasm	
...utrophil ...–7,000 ...m³ blood	10–14 μm in diameter Spherical cells with multilobed nuclei; fine, pink granules in cytoplasm	
...r leukocytes* ...phocyte ...–3,000 ...m³ blood	5–17 μm in diameter (average 9–10 μm) Spherical cells with large, round nuclei	
...nocyte ...700 ...m³ blood	14–24 μm in diameter Large spherical cells with kidney-shaped, round, or lobed nuclei	
...lets (...mbocytes) ...0–500,000 ...m³ blood	Initiate clotting 2–4 μm in diameter Disk-shaped cell fragments with no nuclei; purple granules in cytoplasm	Bone marrow

Plasma	Function	Source
Water (90–92% of plasma)	Maintains blood volume; transports molecules	Absorbed from intestine
Plasma proteins (7–8% of plasma) Albumin Fibrinogen Globulins	Maintain blood osmotic pressure and pH Maintains blood volume and pressure Clotting Transport; fight infection	Liver
Salts (less than 1% of plasma)	Maintain blood osmotic pressure and pH; aid metabolism	Absorbed from intestinal villi
Gases Oxygen Carbon dioxide	Cellular respiration End product of metabolism	Lungs Tissues
Nutrients Fats Glucose Amino acids	Food for cells	Absorbed from intestinal villi
Urea	Nitrogenous waste	Liver
Hormones, vitamins, etc.	Aid metabolism	Varied

*with Wright's stain

Composition of Blood
Figure 36.11

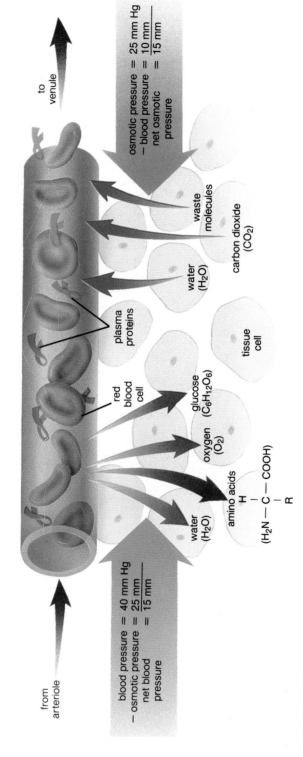

Capillary Exchange
Figure 36.13

from
arteriole

to
venule

blood pressure = 40 mm Hg
— osmotic pressure = 25 mm
net blood   = 15 mm
pressure

osmotic pressure = 25 mm Hg
— blood pressure = 10 mm
net osmotic   = 15 mm
pressure

plasma
proteins

red
blood
cell

water
(H_2O)

oxygen
(O_2)

glucose
($C_6H_{12}O_6$)

amino acids

$(H_2N - C - COOH)$
          $\overset{H}{\underset{R}{|}}$

tissue
cell

water
(H_2O)

carbon dioxide
(CO_2)

waste
molecules

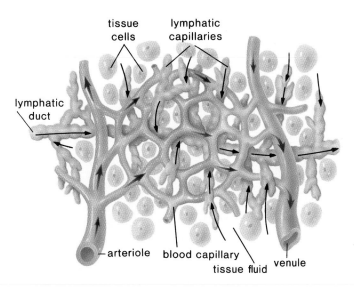

tissue cells

lymphatic capillaries

lymphatic duct

arteriole

blood capillary

tissue fluid

venule

Lymphatic Vessels
Figure 36.14

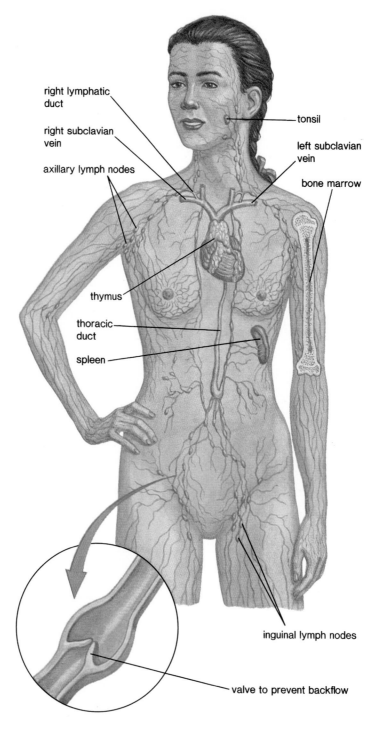

right lymphatic
duct

right subclavian
vein

axillary lymph nodes

thymus

thoracic
duct

spleen

tonsil

left subclavian
vein

bone marrow

inguinal lymph nodes

valve to prevent backflow

Lymphatic Vessel

Lymphatic System
Figure 37.1

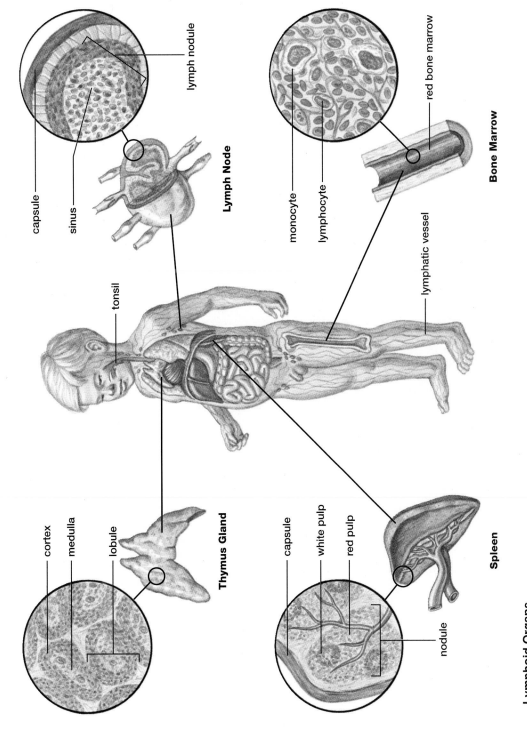

Lymphoid Organs
Figure 37.2

Lymph Node

capsule
sinus
lymph nodule

Bone Marrow

monocyte
lymphocyte
red bone marrow

lymphatic vessel

tonsil

Thymus Gland

cortex
medulla
lobule

Spleen

capsule
white pulp
red pulp
nodule

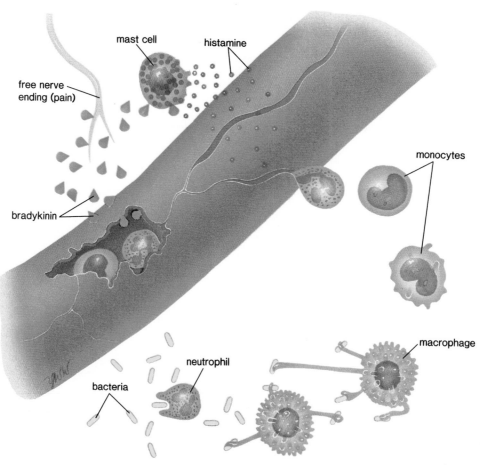

Inflammatory Reaction
Figure 37.4

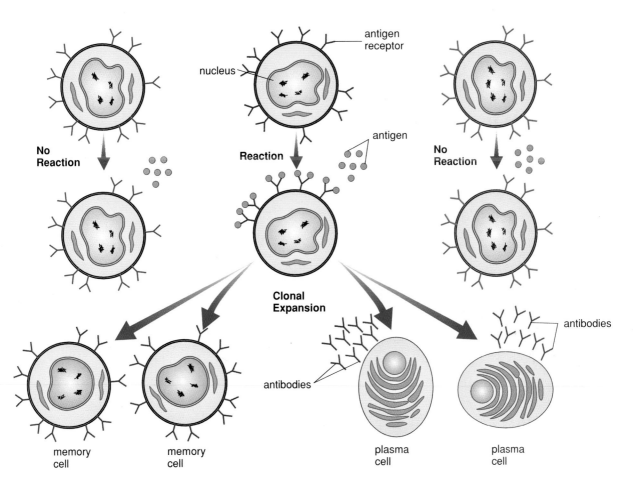

No
Reaction

nucleus

antigen
receptor

Reaction

antigen

No
Reaction

Clonal
Expansion

antibodies

antibodies

memory
cell

memory
cell

plasma
cell

plasma
cell

Clonal Selection Theory
Figure 37.6

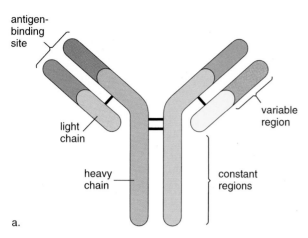

Antigen-Antibody Reaction
Figure 37.7*a*

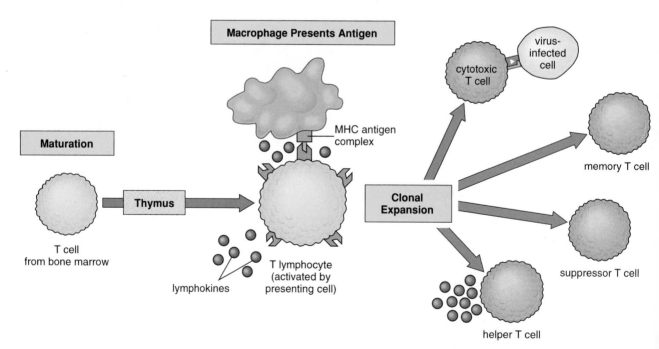

Activation and Diversity of T Cells
Figure 37.9

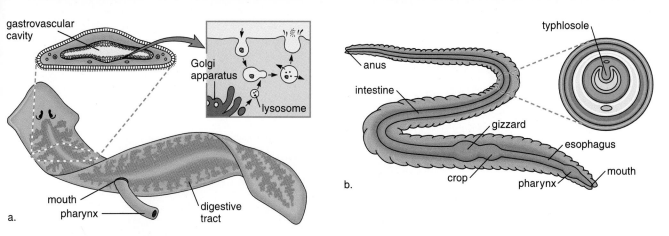

Incomplete vs. Complete Digestive Tract
Figures 38.1 & 38.2

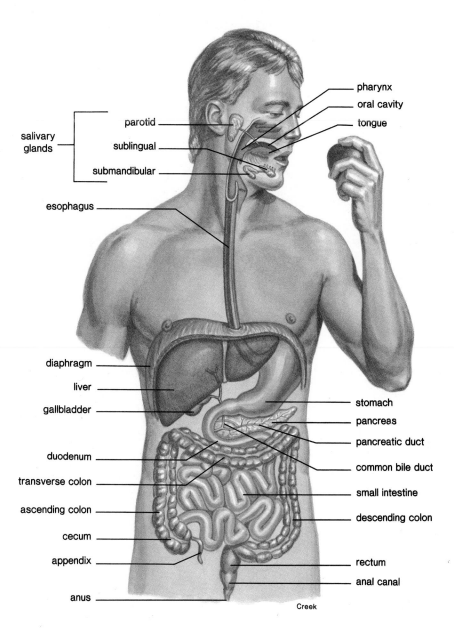

Human Digestive Tract
Figure 38.5

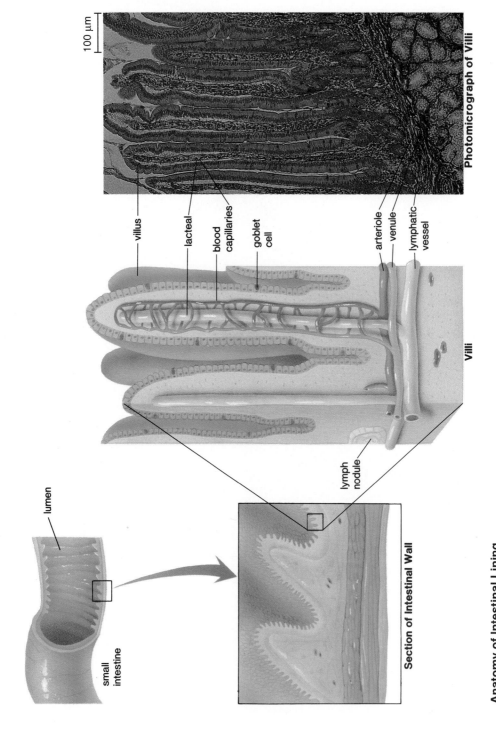

100 μm

Photomicrograph of Villi

villus

lacteal

blood
capillaries

goblet
cell

arteriole
venule
lymphatic
vessel

Villi

lymph
nodule

lumen

small
intestine

Section of Intestinal Wall

Anatomy of Intestinal Lining
Figure 38.9

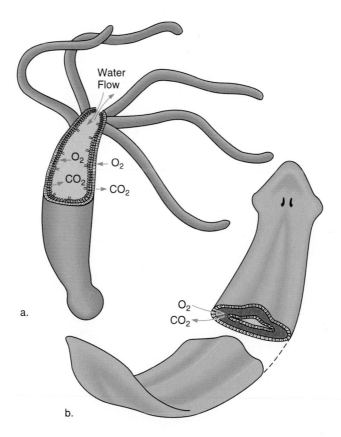

Respiration in Hydras and Planarians
Figure 39.1

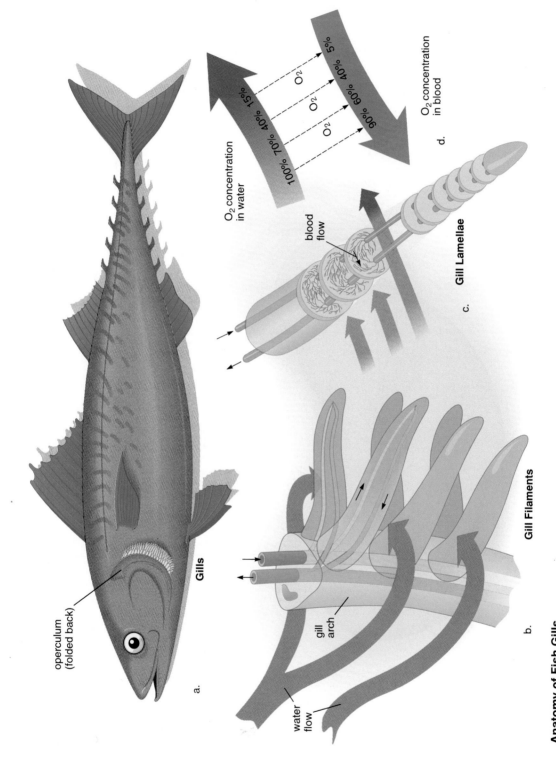

Anatomy of Fish Gills
Figure 39.2

Gills

operculum
(folded back)

a.

gill arch

water flow

Gill Filaments

b.

blood flow

Gill Lamellae

c.

O₂ concentration in water

O^2

O^2

O^2

100% 70% 40% 15%

90% 60% 40% 5%

O₂ concentration in blood

d.

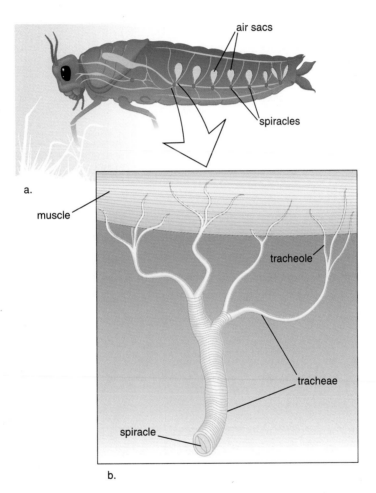

air sacs

spiracles

a.

muscle

tracheole

tracheae

spiracle

b.

Tracheal System of Insects
Figure 39.3

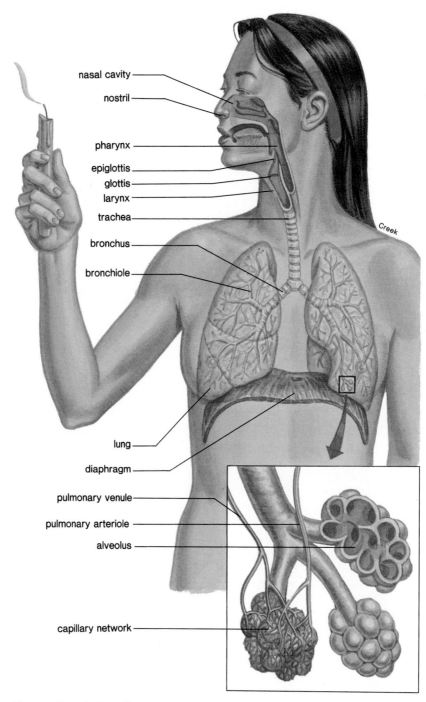

nasal cavity

nostril

pharynx

epiglottis

glottis

larynx

trachea

bronchus

bronchiole

Creek

lung

diaphragm

pulmonary venule

pulmonary arteriole

alveolus

capillary network

Human Respiratory Tract
Figure 39.6

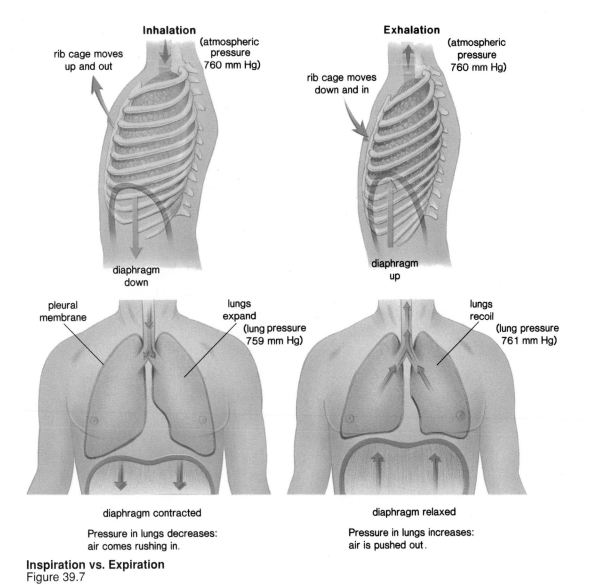

Inhalation

rib cage moves
up and out

(atmospheric
pressure
760 mm Hg)

diaphragm
down

pleural
membrane

lungs
expand
(lung pressure
759 mm Hg)

diaphragm contracted

Pressure in lungs decreases:
air comes rushing in.

Exhalation

(atmospheric
pressure
760 mm Hg)

rib cage moves
down and in

diaphragm
up

lungs
recoil
(lung pressure
761 mm Hg)

diaphragm relaxed

Pressure in lungs increases:
air is pushed out.

Inspiration vs. Expiration
Figure 39.7

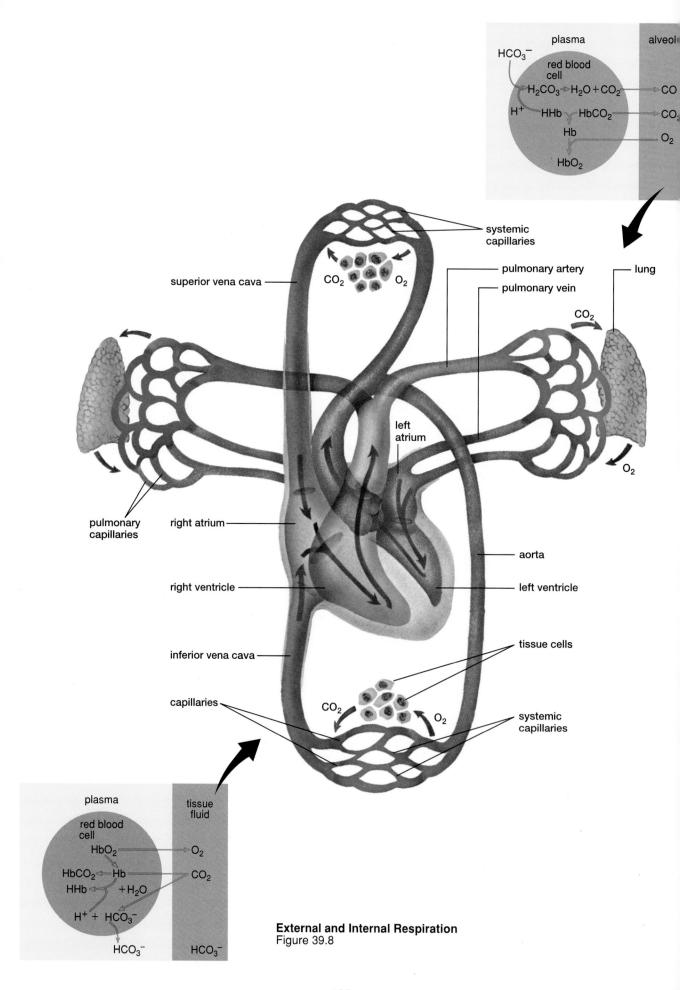

External and Internal Respiration
Figure 39.8

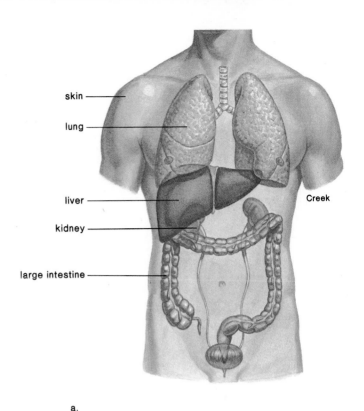

skin

lung

liver

Creek

kidney

large intestine

a.

Excretory Organs
Figure 40.1*a*

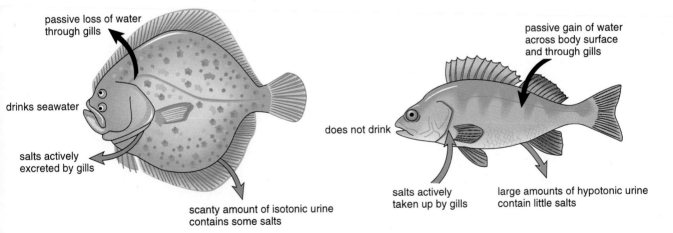

passive loss of water
through gills

drinks seawater

salts actively
excreted by gills

scanty amount of isotonic urine
contains some salts

a. Marine fish

passive gain of water
across body surface
and through gills

does not drink

salts actively
taken up by gills

large amounts of hypotonic urine
contain little salts

b. Freshwater fish

Water and Salt Balance in Bony Fishes
Figure 40.3

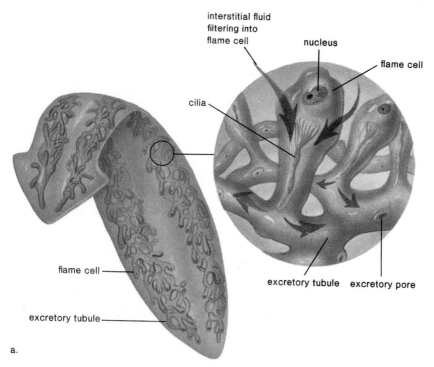

Planarian Flame Cell Excretory System
Figure 40.4*a*

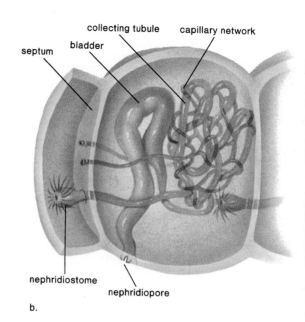

Earthworm Nephridium Excretory System
Figure 40.4*b*

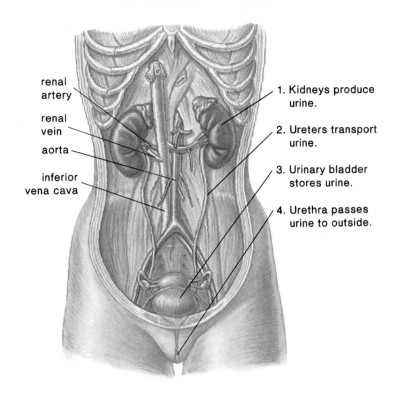

renal
artery

renal
vein

aorta

inferior
vena cava

1. Kidneys produce urine.

2. Ureters transport urine.

3. Urinary bladder stores urine.

4. Urethra passes urine to outside.

Urinary System in Humans
Figure 40.5

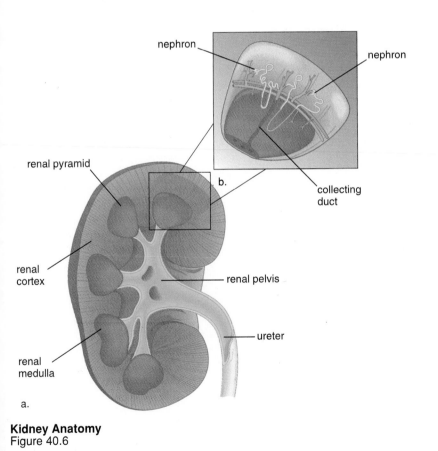

nephron

nephron

renal pyramid

b.

collecting duct

renal cortex

renal pelvis

renal medulla

ureter

a.

Kidney Anatomy
Figure 40.6

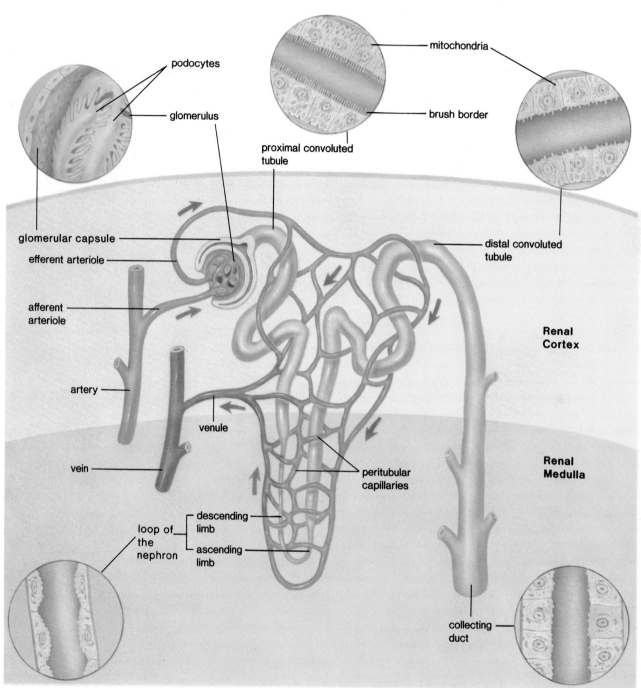

Nephron Anatomy
Figure 40.7

podocytes

glomerulus

mitochondria

brush border

proximal convoluted
tubule

glomerular capsule

efferent arteriole

distal convoluted
tubule

afferent
arteriole

**Renal
Cortex**

artery

venule

vein

peritubular
capillaries

**Renal
Medulla**

loop of
the
nephron

descending
limb

ascending
limb

collecting
duct

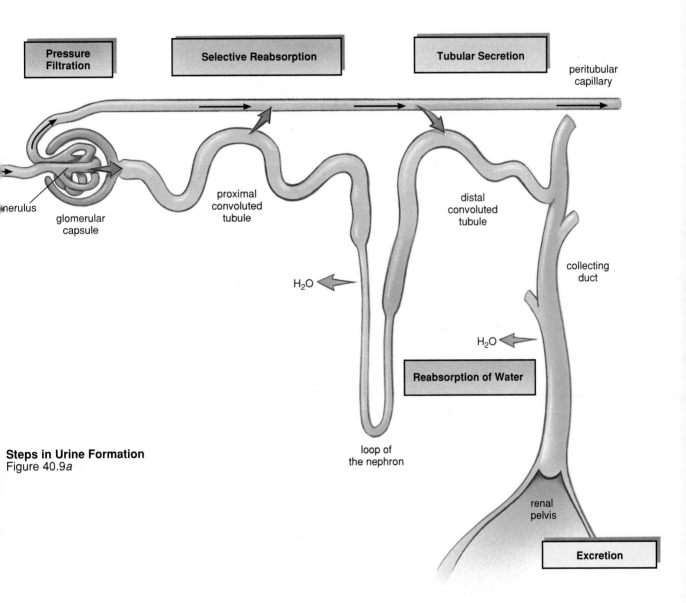

Pressure Filtration

Selective Reabsorption

Tubular Secretion

peritubular capillary

merulus

glomerular capsule

proximal convoluted tubule

distal convoluted tubule

collecting duct

H_2O

H_2O

Reabsorption of Water

loop of the nephron

renal pelvis

Excretion

Steps in Urine Formation
Figure 40.9a

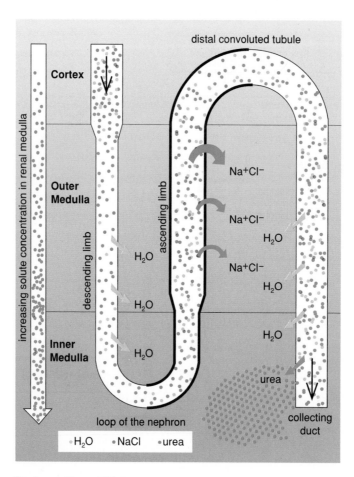

Reabsorption of Water
Figure 40.10

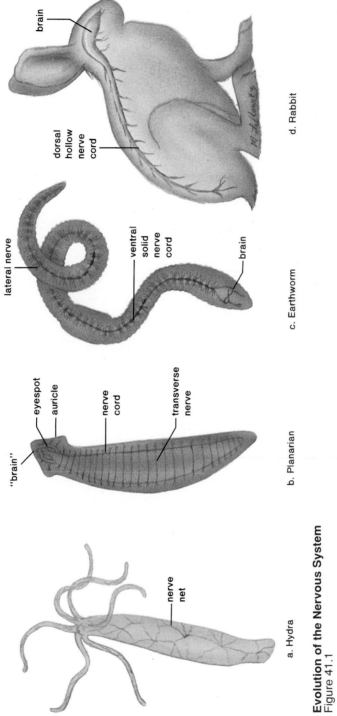

Evolution of the Nervous System
Figure 41.1

a. Hydra

nerve net

b. Planarian

"brain"
eyespot
auricle
nerve cord
transverse nerve

c. Earthworm

lateral nerve
ventral solid nerve cord
brain

d. Rabbit

brain
dorsal hollow nerve cord

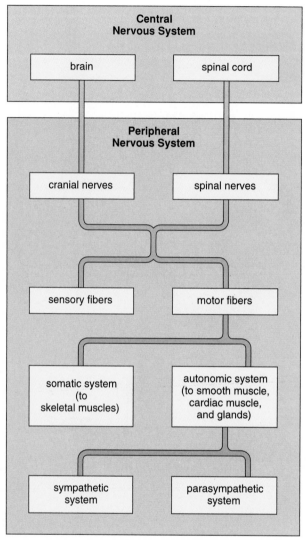

b.

Organization of the Human Nervous System
Figure 41.2*b*

d. Parts of a neuron

Name	Function
Dendrite	A fiber that receives information and generally conducts nerve impulses to the cell body.
Cell body	Contains the nucleus and other organelles and manufactures neurotransmitters.
Axon	A fiber that conducts nerve impulses away from the cell body and releases neurotransmitters.

Both integrate (sum up excitatory and inhibitory inputs.

cell body

receptor cell

dendrite

neurolemmal node

myelin sheath

cell body

axon

a. Motor neuron

dendrite

cell body

axon

b. Sensory neuron

c. Interneuron

Neuron Anatomy
Figure 41.3

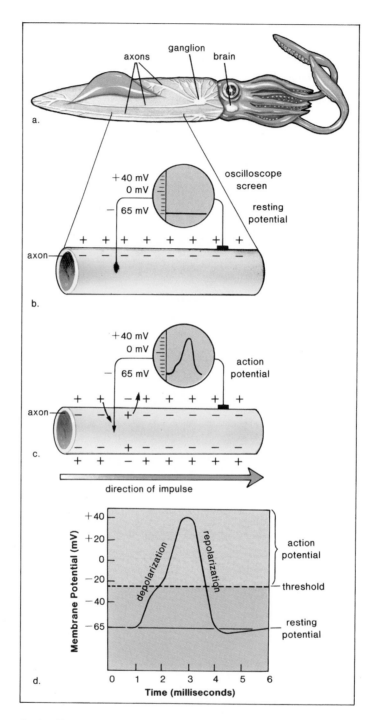

Action Potential (Voltage Changes)
Figure 41.4*a-d*

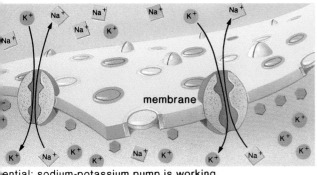

ential: sodium-potassium pump is working.

When a neuron is not conducting a nerve impulse, the sodium (Na⁺) and potassium (K⁺) gates are closed. The sodium-potassium pump maintains the uneven distribution of these ions across the membrane. The oscilloscope registers a resting potential of −65 mV inside compared to outside.

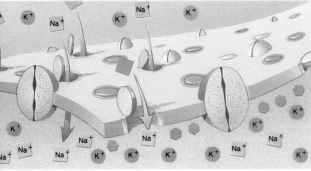

ntial: sodium gates are open.

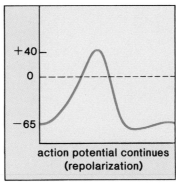

An action potential begins when the sodium gates open and sodium ions move to the inside. The oscilloscope registers a depolarization as the cytoplasm reaches +40 mV compared to tissue fluid.

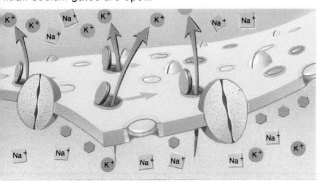

ntial: potassium gates are open.

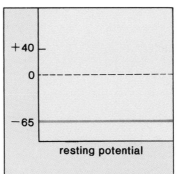

The action potential continues as the sodium gates close and the potassium gates open, allowing potassium ions to move to the outside. The oscilloscope registers repolarization as the cytoplasm again becomes −65 mV compared to tissue fluid.

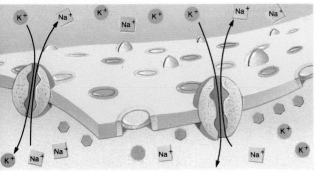

period: sodium-potassium pump is working.

The oscilloscope registers −65 mV again, but the sodium-potassium pump is working to restore the original sodium and potassium ion distribution. The sodium and potassium gates are now closed but will open again in response to another stimulus.

Action Potential and Resting Potential
Figure 41.5

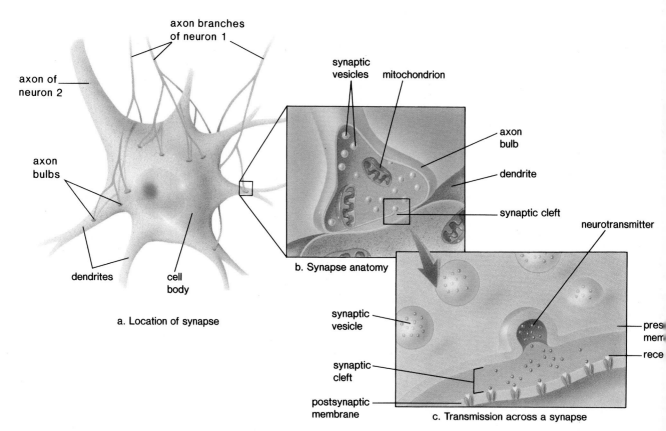

a. Location of synapse

b. Synapse anatomy

c. Transmission across a synapse

Synapse Structure and Function
Figure 41.7

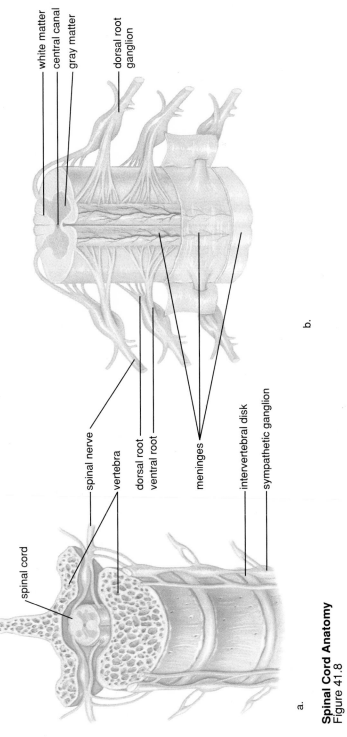

white matter
central canal
gray matter
dorsal root ganglion

spinal nerve
vertebra
dorsal root
ventral root
meninges
intervertebral disk
sympathetic ganglion

spinal cord

a.

b.

Spinal Cord Anatomy
Figure 41.8

203

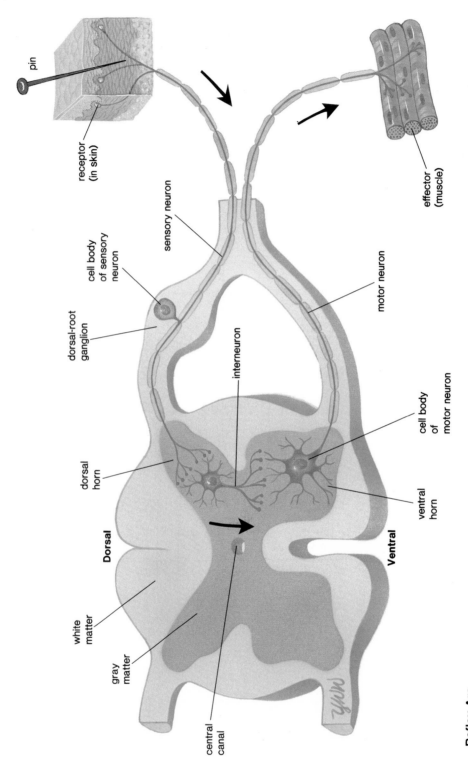

Reflex Arc
Figure 41.9

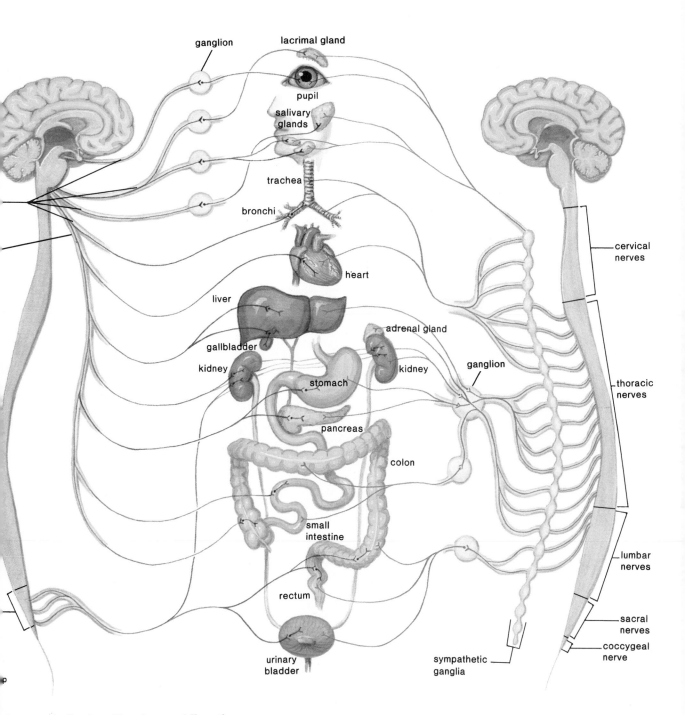

ganglion
lacrimal gland
pupil
salivary glands
trachea
bronchi
heart
liver
adrenal gland
gallbladder
kidney
kidney
ganglion
stomach
pancreas
colon
small intestine
rectum
urinary bladder
sympathetic ganglia

cervical nerves
thoracic nerves
lumbar nerves
sacral nerves
coccygeal nerve

Autonomic System Structure and Function
Figure 41.10

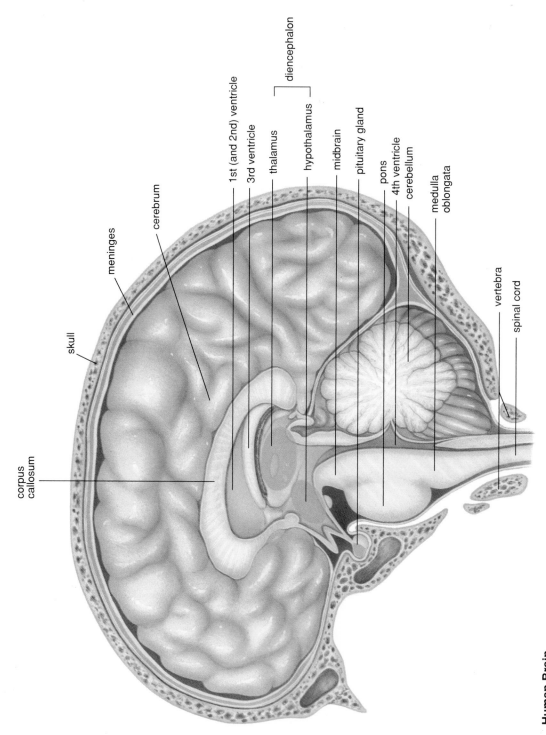

Human Brain
Figure 41.12

Labels: diencephalon · 1st (and 2nd) ventricle · 3rd ventricle · thalamus · hypothalamus · midbrain · pituitary gland · pons · 4th ventricle · cerebellum · medulla oblongata · meninges · cerebrum · skull · corpus callosum · vertebra · spinal cord

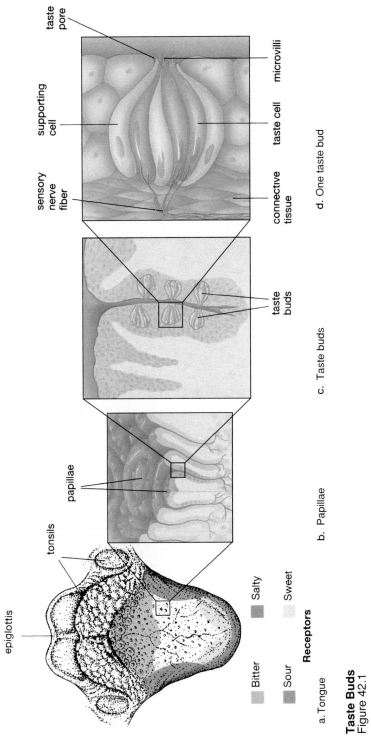

taste
pore

microvilli

supporting
cell

taste cell

sensory
nerve
fiber

connective
tissue

d. One taste bud

taste
buds

c. Taste buds

papillae

b. Papillae

tonsils

epiglottis

Receptors

Bitter   Salty

Sour   Sweet

a. Tongue

Taste Buds
Figure 42.1

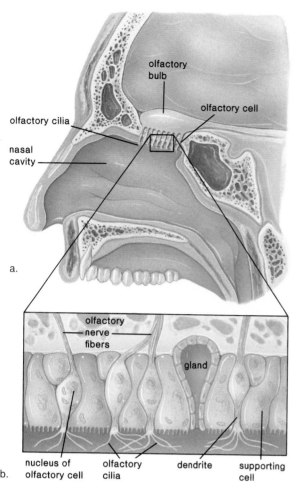

Olfactory Cell Location and Anatomy
Figure 42.2

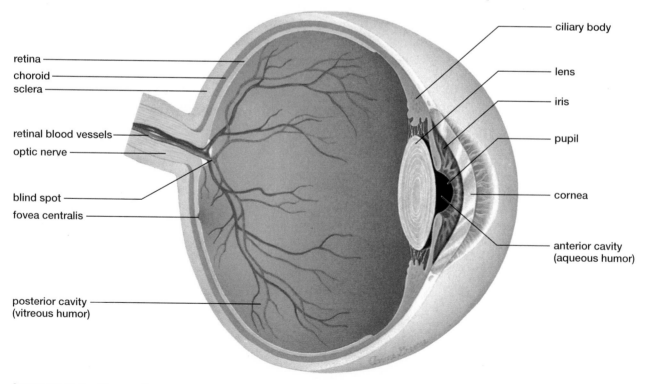

Anatomy of the Human Eye
Figure 42.5

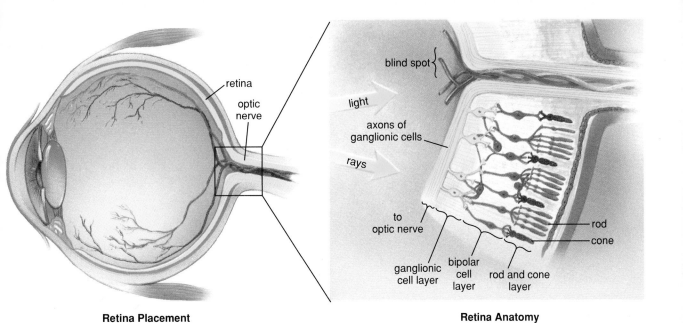

Retina Placement

Retina Anatomy

Anatomy of the Retina
Figure 42.6

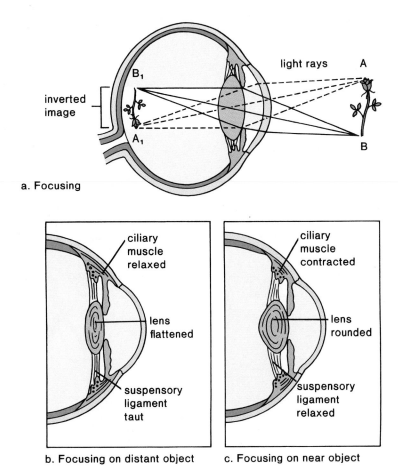

a. Focusing

b. Focusing on distant object   c. Focusing on near object

Focusing
Figure 42.7

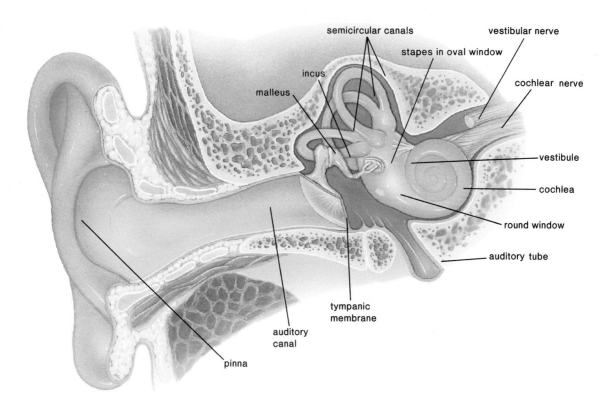

Anatomy of the Human Ear
Figure 42.10

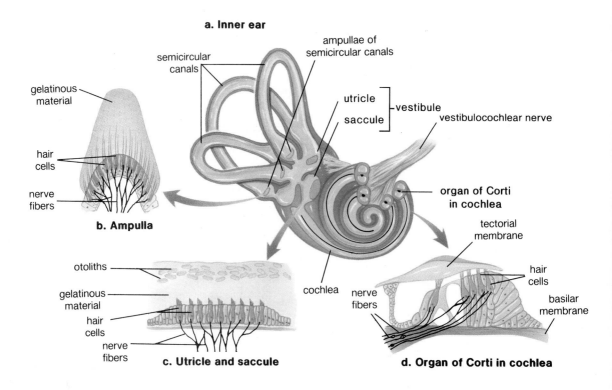

Anatomy of the Inner Ear
Figure 42.11

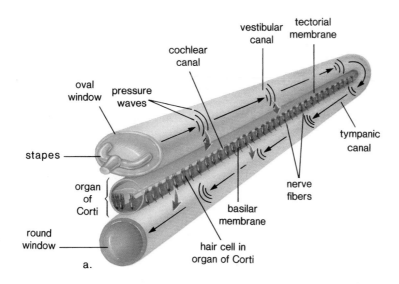

Unwound Cochlea
Figure 42.13*a*

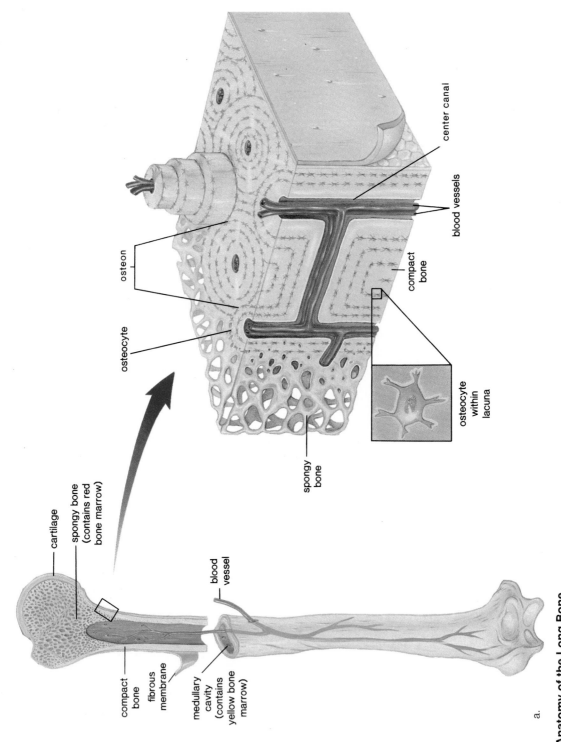

center canal

blood vessels

compact bone

osteocyte within lacuna

spongy bone

osteon

osteocyte

cartilage

spongy bone (contains red bone marrow)

compact bone

fibrous membrane

blood vessel

medullary cavity (contains yellow bone marrow)

Anatomy of the Long Bone
Figure 43.4a

a.

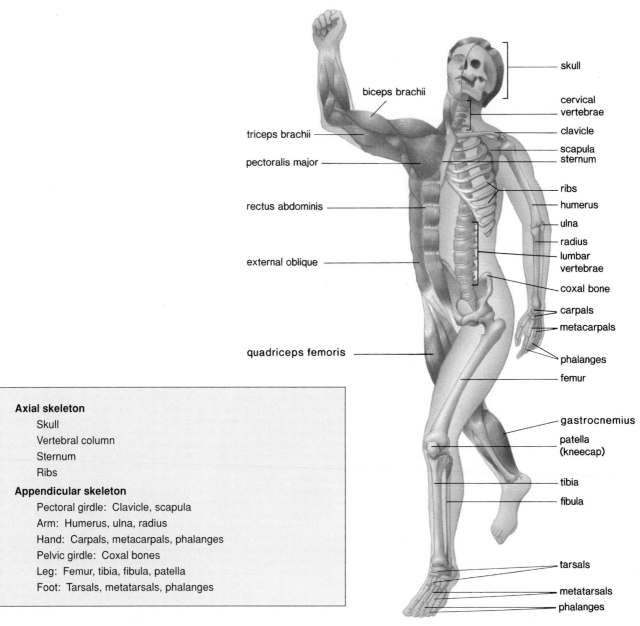

skull

biceps brachii

triceps brachii

pectoralis major

rectus abdominis

external oblique

quadriceps femoris

cervical
vertebrae

clavicle

scapula
sternum

ribs

humerus

ulna

radius

lumbar
vertebrae

coxal bone

carpals

metacarpals

phalanges

femur

gastrocnemius

patella
(kneecap)

tibia

fibula

tarsals

metatarsals

phalanges

Axial skeleton
  Skull
  Vertebral column
  Sternum
  Ribs
Appendicular skeleton
  Pectoral girdle: Clavicle, scapula
  Arm: Humerus, ulna, radius
  Hand: Carpals, metacarpals, phalanges
  Pelvic girdle: Coxal bones
  Leg: Femur, tibia, fibula, patella
  Foot: Tarsals, metatarsals, phalanges

Human Skeleton and Major Muscles
Figure 43.5

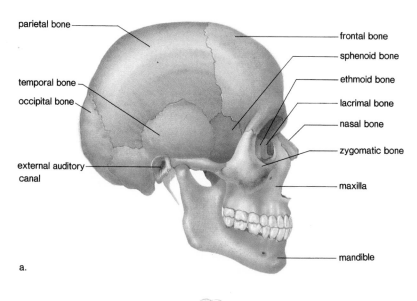

parietal bone

frontal bone

sphenoid bone

ethmoid bone

temporal bone

lacrimal bone

occipital bone

nasal bone

zygomatic bone

external auditory canal

maxilla

mandible

a.

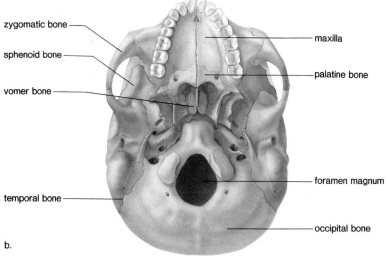

zygomatic bone

maxilla

sphenoid bone

palatine bone

vomer bone

temporal bone

foramen magnum

occipital bone

b.

Skull
Figure 43.6

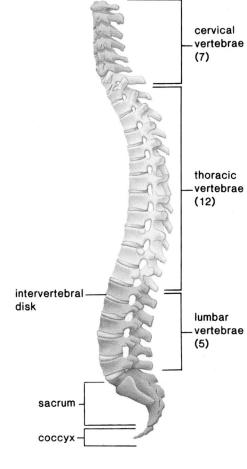

Vertebral Column
Figure 43.7

cervical
vertebrae
(7)

thoracic
vertebrae
(12)

intervertebral
disk

lumbar
vertebrae
(5)

sacrum

coccyx

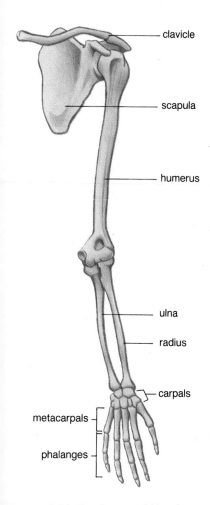

clavicle

scapula

humerus

ulna

radius

carpals

metacarpals

phalanges

Pectoral Girdle, Arm, and Hand
Figure 43.8

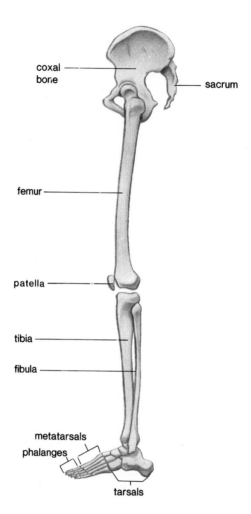

Pelvic Girdle, Legs, and Foot
Figure 43.9

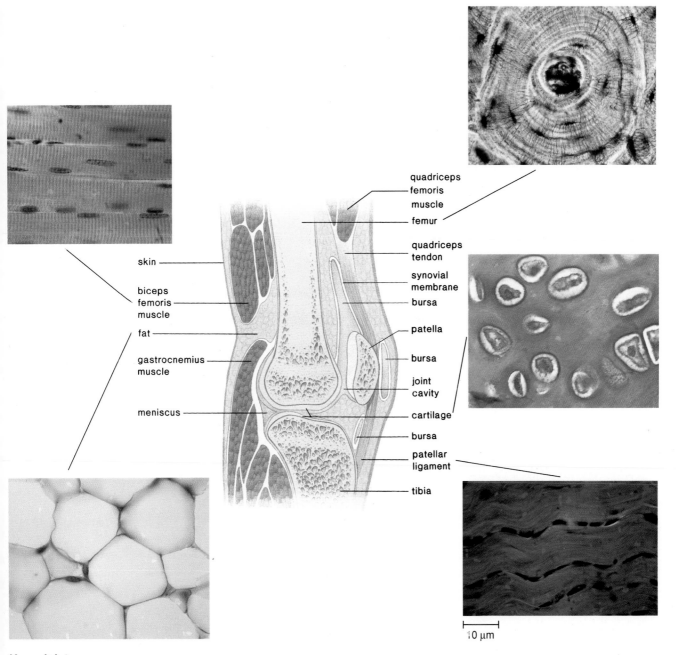

quadriceps
femoris
muscle

femur

skin

quadriceps
tendon

synovial
membrane

biceps
femoris
muscle

bursa

fat

patella

gastrocnemius
muscle

bursa

joint
cavity

meniscus

cartilage

bursa

patellar
ligament

tibia

10 µm

Knee Joint
Figure 43.10

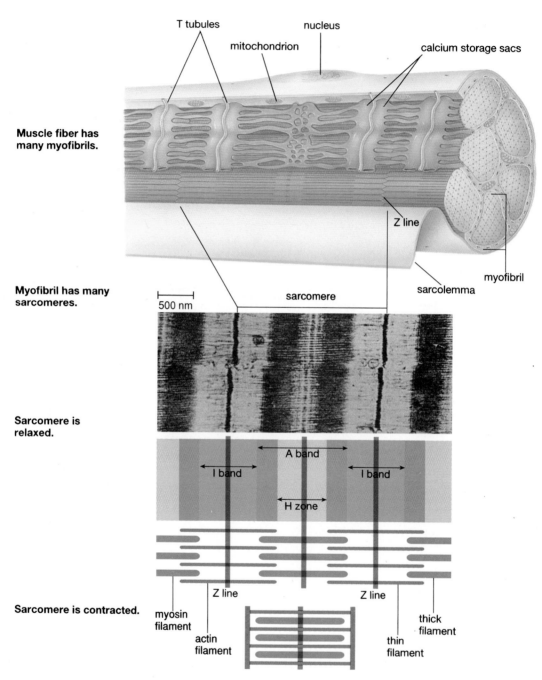

T tubules   nucleus

mitochondrion   calcium storage sacs

Muscle fiber has many myofibrils.

Z line

myofibril

sarcolemma

Myofibril has many sarcomeres.

sarcomere

500 nm

Sarcomere is relaxed.

A band

I band   I band

H zone

Z line   Z line

Sarcomere is contracted.

myosin filament

actin filament

thick filament

thin filament

Skeletal Muscle Fiber Structure and Function
Figure 43.13

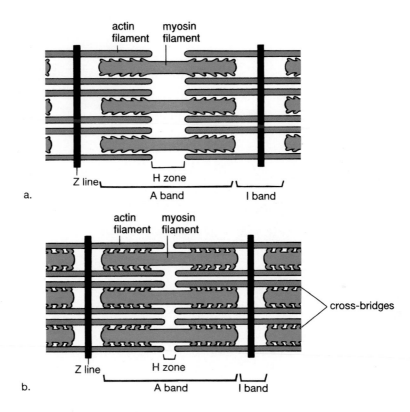

Sliding Filament Theory
Figure 43.14

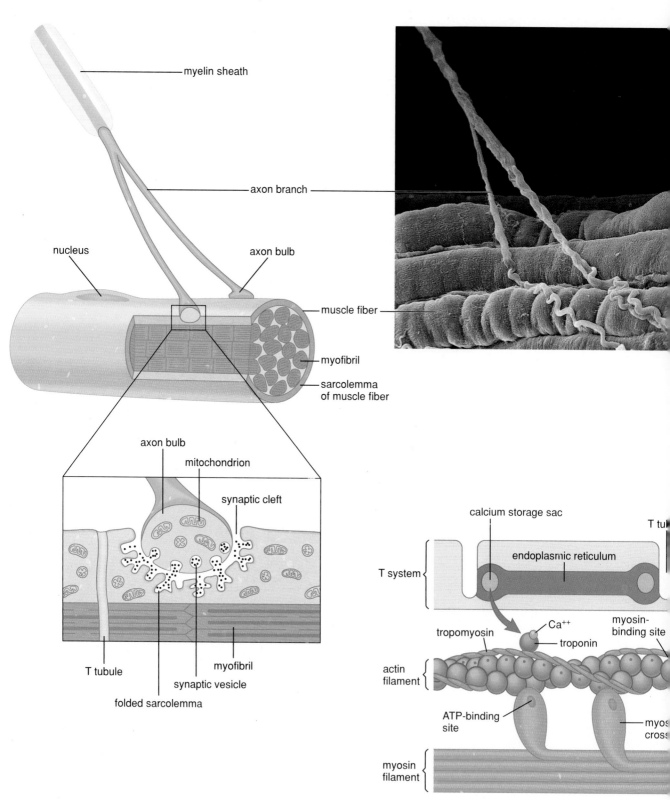

myelin sheath

axon branch

nucleus

axon bulb

muscle fiber

myofibril

sarcolemma
of muscle fiber

axon bulb

mitochondrion

synaptic cleft

calcium storage sac

T tu

endoplasmic reticulum

T system

tropomyosin

Ca^{++}

myosin-
binding site

troponin

actin
filament

T tubule

myofibril

ATP-binding
site

synaptic vesicle

folded sarcolemma

myos
cross

myosin
filament

Neuromuscular Junction
Figure 43.15

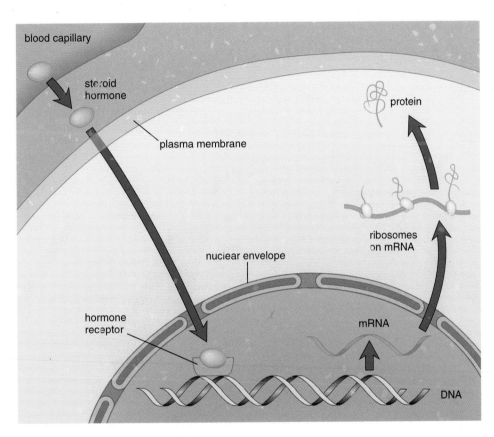

Cellular Activity of Steroid Hormones
Figure 44.1

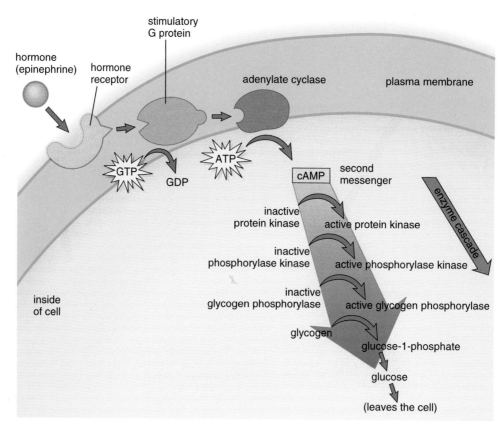

Cellular Activity of Peptide Hormones
Figure 44.2

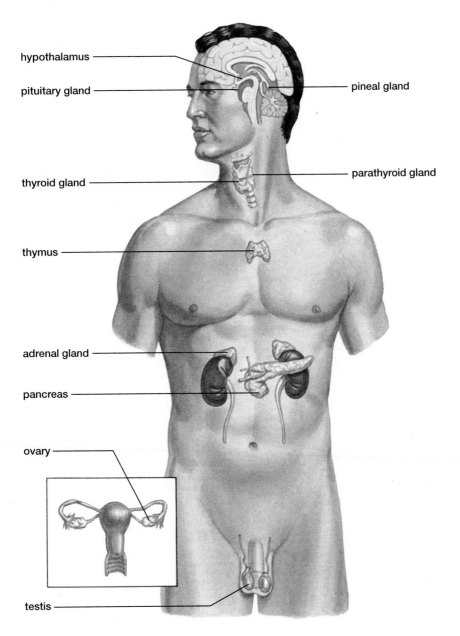

hypothalamus

pituitary gland

pineal gland

parathyroid gland

thyroid gland

thymus

adrenal gland

pancreas

ovary

testis

Human Endocrine System
Figure 44.3

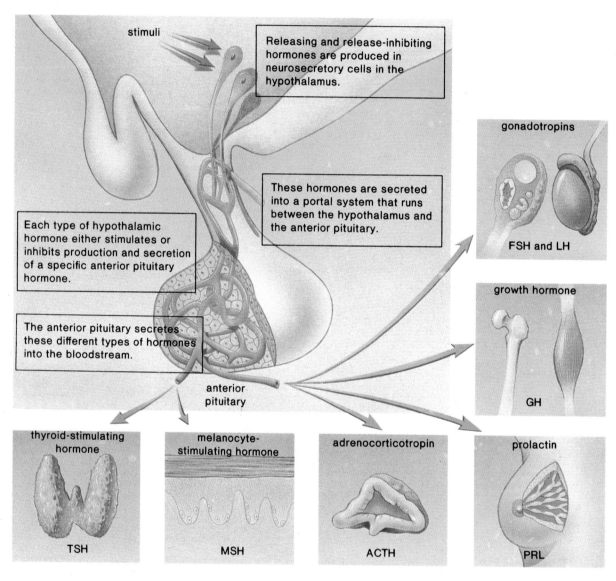

stimuli

Releasing and release-inhibiting hormones are produced in neurosecretory cells in the hypothalamus.

These hormones are secreted into a portal system that runs between the hypothalamus and the anterior pituitary.

Each type of hypothalamic hormone either stimulates or inhibits production and secretion of a specific anterior pituitary hormone.

The anterior pituitary secretes these different types of hormones into the bloodstream.

anterior pituitary

gonadotropins

FSH and LH

growth hormone

GH

thyroid-stimulating hormone

TSH

melanocyte-stimulating hormone

MSH

adrenocorticotropin

ACTH

prolactin

PRL

Hypothalamus and Anterior Pituitary
Figure 44.4

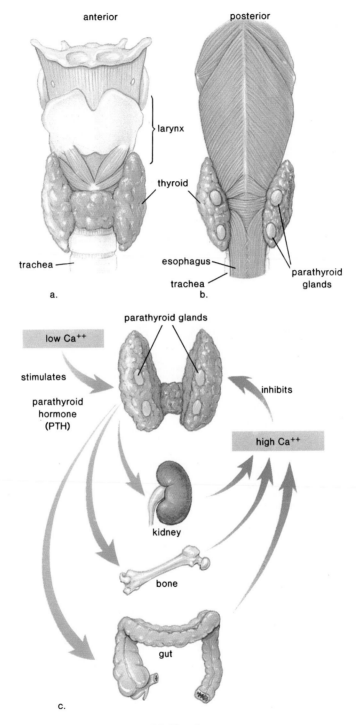

anterior

posterior

larynx

thyroid

trachea

esophagus

trachea

parathyroid glands

a.

b.

parathyroid glands

low Ca++

stimulates

parathyroid hormone (PTH)

inhibits

high Ca++

kidney

bone

gut

c.

Thyroid and Parathyroid Glands
Figure 44.5

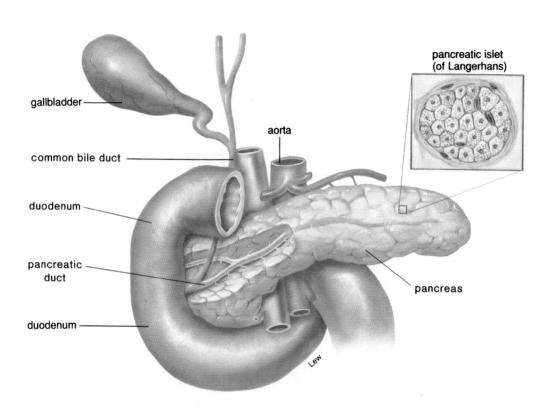

gallbladder

common bile duct

duodenum

pancreatic
duct

duodenum

aorta

pancreatic islet
(of Langerhans)

pancreas

Lew

Steps	Example
Identify the source of the chemical	Pancreas is source
Identify the effect to be studied	Presence of pancreas in body lowers blood sugar
Isolate the chemical	Insulin isolated from pancreatic secretions
Show that the chemical alone has the effect	Insulin alone lowers blood sugar

The Pancreas as Endocrine/Exocrine Gland
Figure 44.7

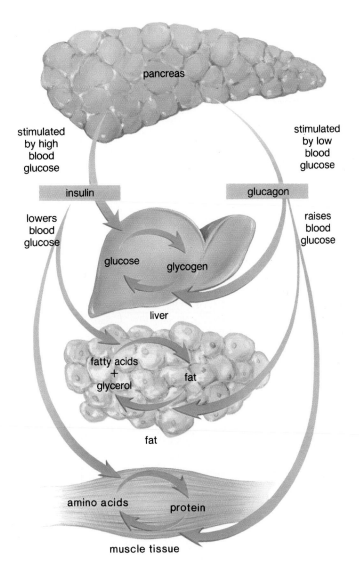

Insulin and Glucagon Homeostatic System
Figure 44.8

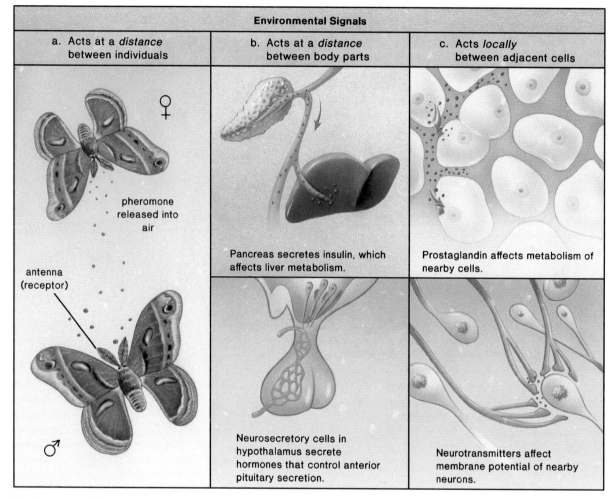

Environmental Signals		
a. Acts at a *distance* between individuals	**b. Acts at a *distance* between body parts**	**c. Acts *locally* between adjacent cells**
♀ pheromone released into air antenna (receptor) ♂	Pancreas secretes insulin, which affects liver metabolism. Neurosecretory cells in hypothalamus secrete hormones that control anterior pituitary secretion.	Prostaglandin affects metabolism of nearby cells. Neurotransmitters affect membrane potential of nearby neurons.

Environmental Signals
Figure 44.9

clitellum

testes

sperm duct
ovary
seminal vesicle

seminal receptacle

a.

anterior end

clitellum

clitellum

anterior end

b.

Reproduction in Earthworms
Figure 45.2

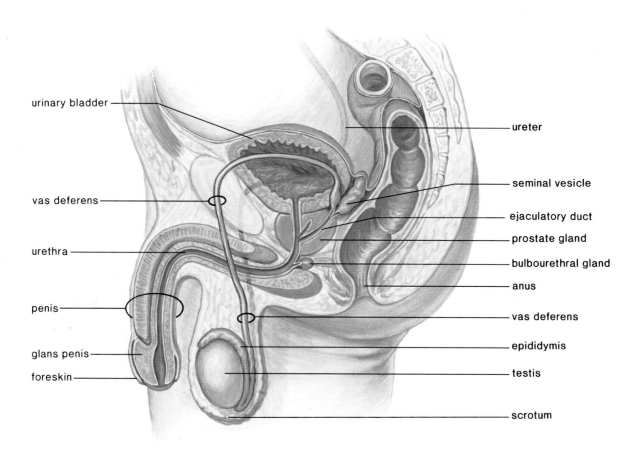

urinary bladder

ureter

vas deferens

seminal vesicle

ejaculatory duct

urethra

prostate gland

bulbourethral gland

penis

anus

vas deferens

glans penis

epididymis

foreskin

testis

scrotum

Male Reproductive System
Figure 45.5

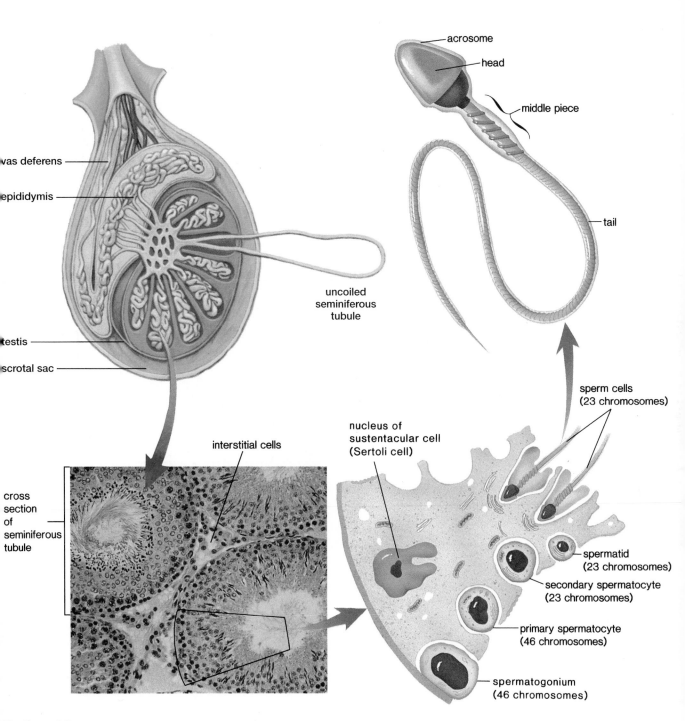

acrosome

head

middle piece

vas deferens

epididymis

tail

testis

scrotal sac

uncoiled
seminiferous
tubule

sperm cells
(23 chromosomes)

interstitial cells

nucleus of
sustentacular cell
(Sertoli cell)

cross
section
of
seminiferous
tubule

spermatid
(23 chromosomes)

secondary spermatocyte
(23 chromosomes)

primary spermatocyte
(46 chromosomes)

spermatogonium
(46 chromosomes)

Testis and Sperm
Figure 45.7

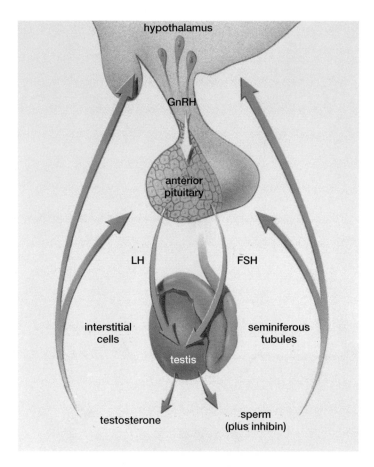

Hypothalamus-Pituitary-Testis Control Relationship
Figure 45.8

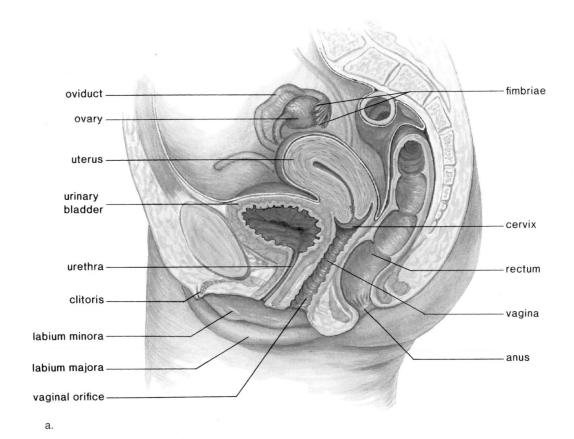

oviduct

ovary

uterus

urinary
bladder

urethra

clitoris

labium minora

labium majora

vaginal orifice

fimbriae

cervix

rectum

vagina

anus

a.

Female Reproductive System
Figure 45.9*a*

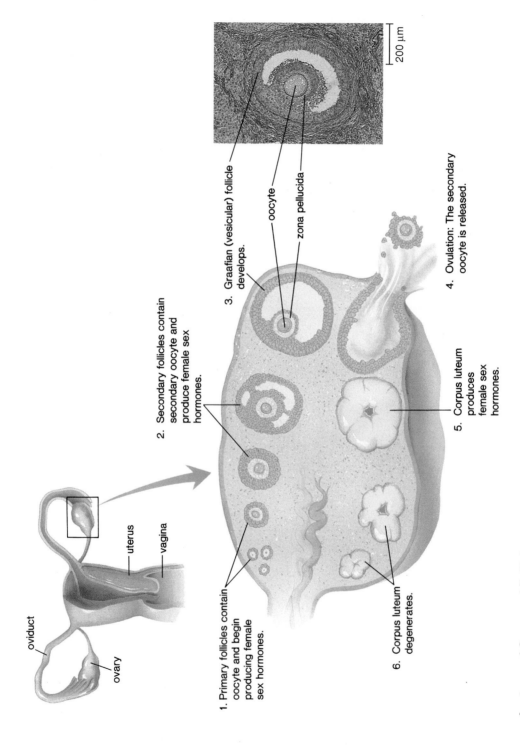

oviduct

uterus

vagina

ovary

200 μm

3. Graafian (vesicular) follicle develops.

oocyte

zona pellucida

4. Ovulation: The secondary oocyte is released.

2. Secondary follicles contain secondary oocyte and produce female sex hormones.

5. Corpus luteum produces female sex hormones.

1. Primary follicles contain oocyte and begin producing female sex hormones.

6. Corpus luteum degenerates.

Anatomy of Ovary and Follicle
Figure 45.10

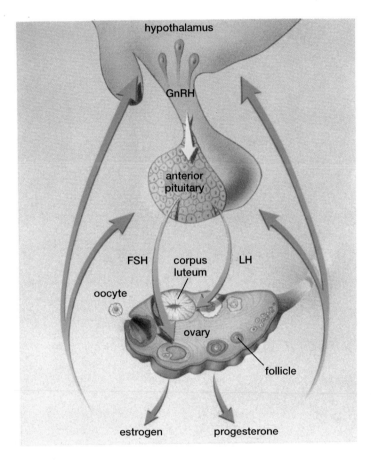

Hypothalamic-Pituitary-Ovary Control Relationship
Figure 45.11

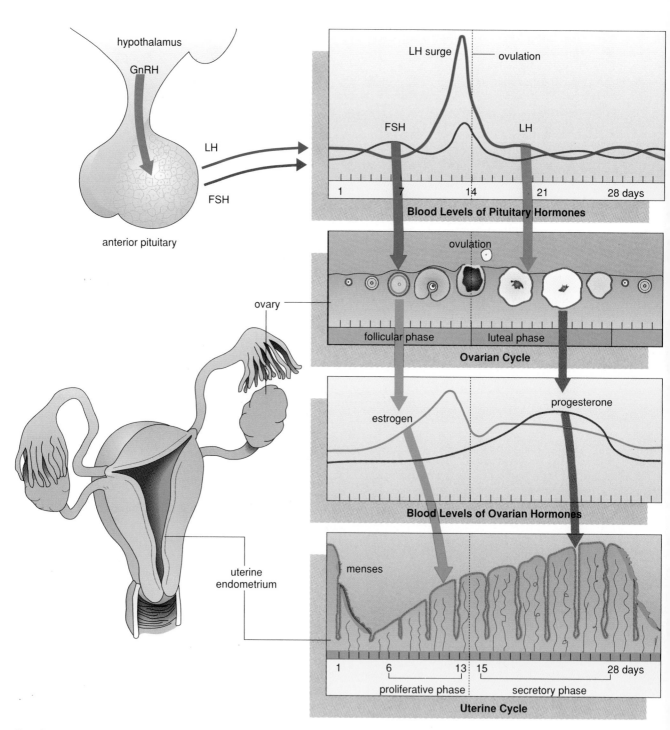

hypothalamus

GnRH

LH

FSH

anterior pituitary

LH surge — ovulation

FSH

LH

1   7   14   21   28 days

Blood Levels of Pituitary Hormones

ovary

ovulation

follicular phase   luteal phase

Ovarian Cycle

estrogen   progesterone

Blood Levels of Ovarian Hormones

uterine
endometrium

menses

1   6   13 15   28 days

proliferative phase   secretory phase

Uterine Cycle

Ovarian and Uterine Cycles
Figure 45.12

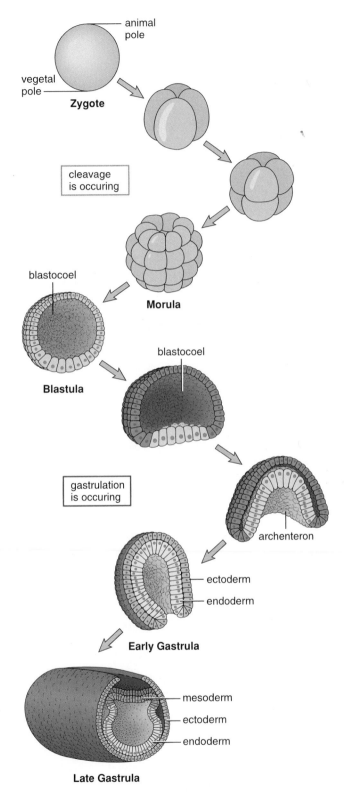

Early Development in Lancelet
Figure 46.2

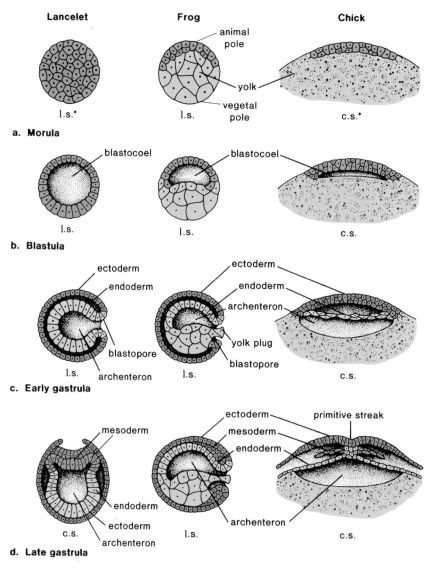

Lancelet **Frog** **Chick**

animal
pole

yolk

vegetal
pole

l.s.*   l.s.   c.s.*

a. Morula

blastocoel   blastocoel

l.s.   l.s.   c.s.

b. Blastula

ectoderm   ectoderm

endoderm   endoderm

archenteron

yolk plug

blastopore   blastopore

l.s.   archenteron   l.s.   c.s.

c. Early gastrula

mesoderm   ectoderm   primitive streak

mesoderm

endoderm

endoderm

ectoderm   archenteron

c.s.   l.s.   c.s.

archenteron

d. Late gastrula

*l.s. = longitudinal section; c.s. = cross section

Comparative Stages of Development
Figure 46.3

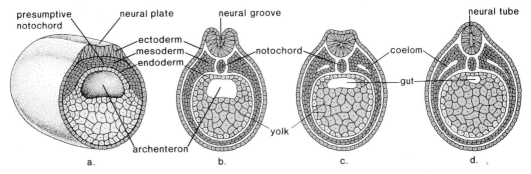

Development of Neural Tube and Coelom
Figure 46.4

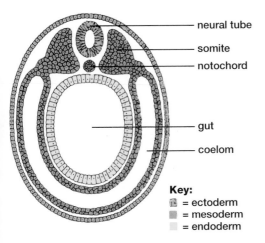

Key:
▓ = ectoderm
▒ = mesoderm
░ = endoderm

Chordate Embryo at Neurula Stage, C.S
Figure 46.5

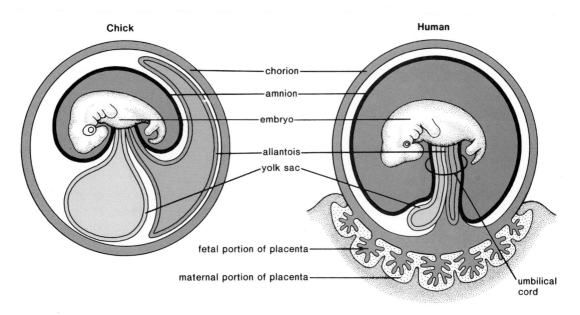

Extraembryonic Membranes
Figure 46.9

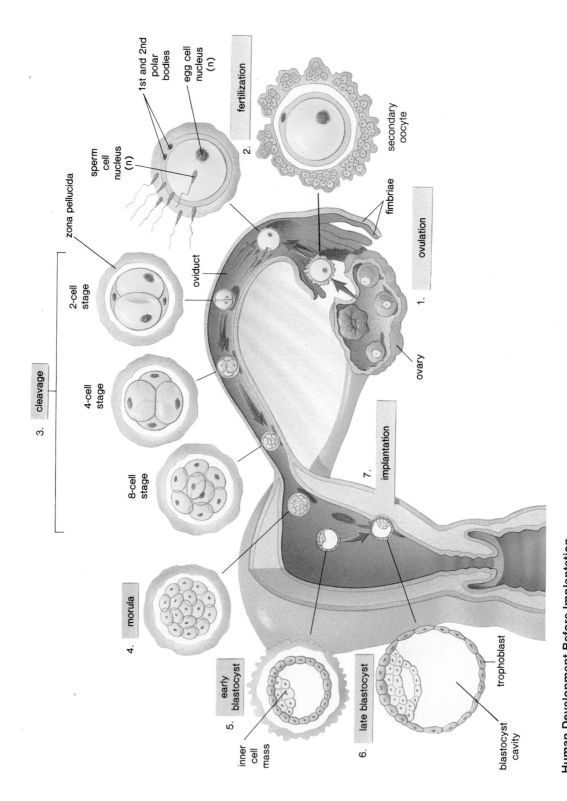

Human Development Before Implantation
Figure 46.10

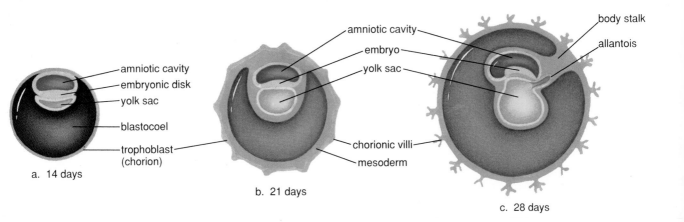

amniotic cavity
embryonic disk
yolk sac
blastocoel
trophoblast (chorion)

a. 14 days

amniotic cavity
embryo
yolk sac

chorionic villi
mesoderm

b. 21 days

body stalk
allantois

amniotic cavity
embryo
yolk sac

c. 28 days

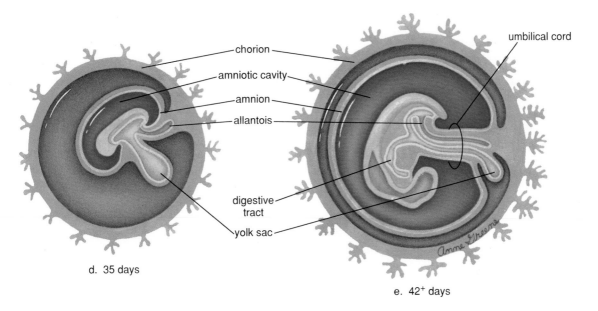

chorion
amniotic cavity
amnion
allantois

digestive tract
yolk sac

d. 35 days

umbilical cord

e. 42+ days

Early Development of Human Embryo
Figure 46.11

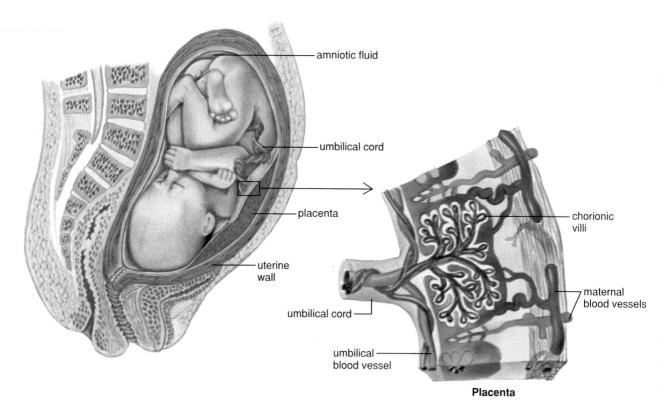

amniotic fluid

umbilical cord

placenta

uterine
wall

chorionic
villi

maternal
blood vessels

umbilical cord

umbilical
blood vessel

Placenta

Placenta Anatomy
Figure 46.13

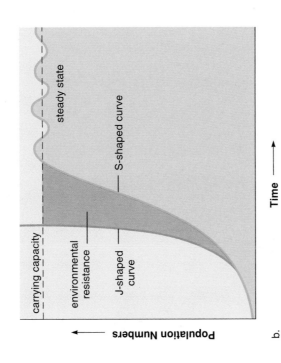

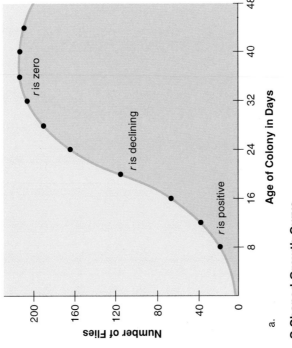

S-Shaped Growth Curve
Figure 48.2

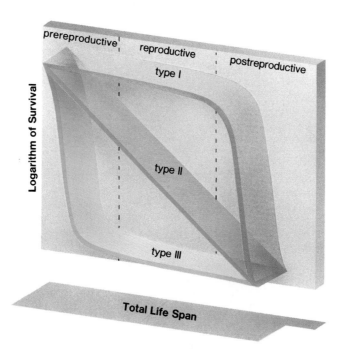

Survivorship Curves
Figure 48.4

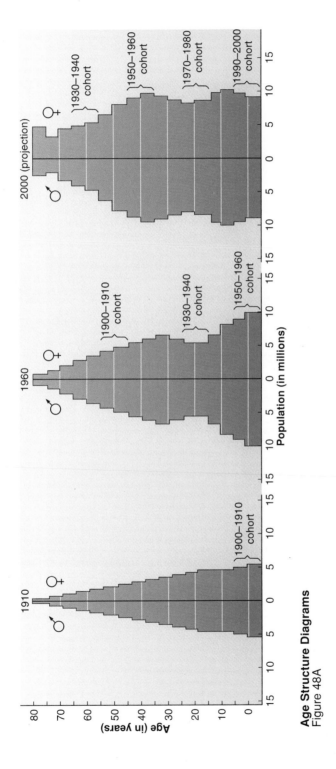

Age Structure Diagrams
Figure 48A

a.

Ecosystem Composition
Figure 50.1a

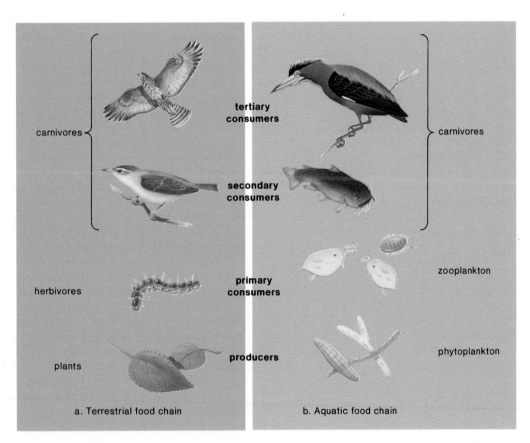

carnivores {	tertiary consumers		carnivores
	secondary consumers		
herbivores	primary consumers		zooplankton
plants	producers		phytoplankton

a. Terrestrial food chain   b. Aquatic food chain

Examples of Food Chains
Figure 50.4

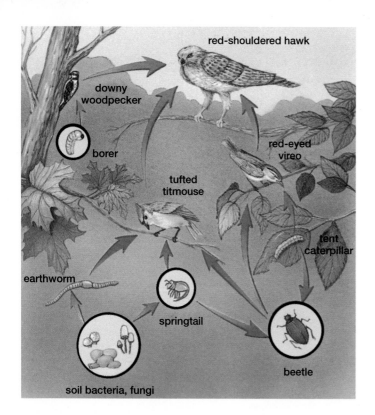

Deciduous Forest Ecosystem
Figure 50.5

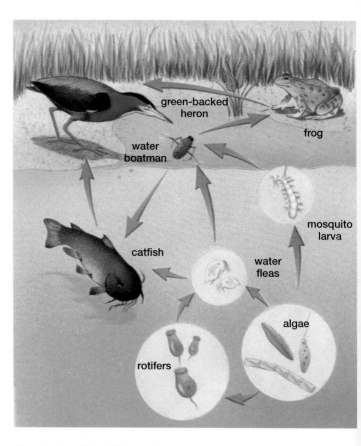

Freshwater Pond Ecosystem
Figure 50.6

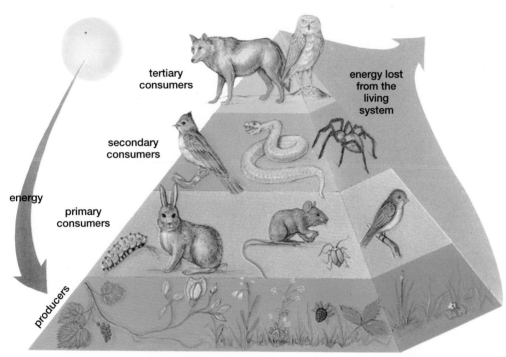

tertiary
consumers

energy lost
from the
living
system

secondary
consumers

energy

primary
consumers

producers

energy retained in the
living system

Pyramid of Energy
Figure 50.7

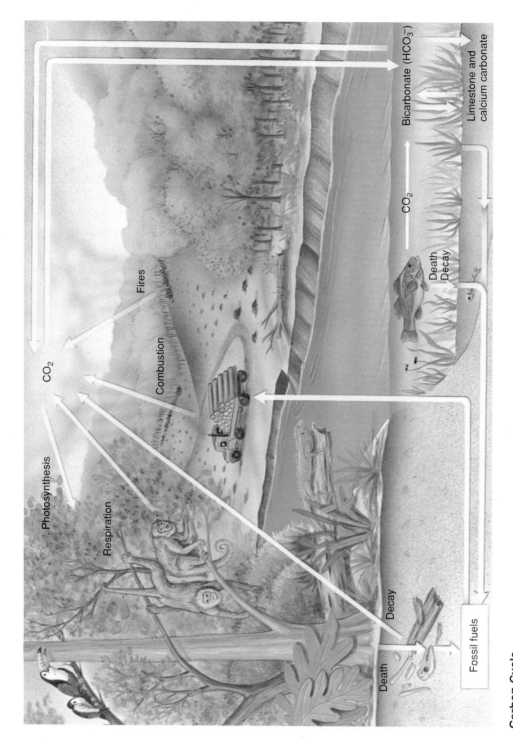

Carbon Cycle
Figure 50.9

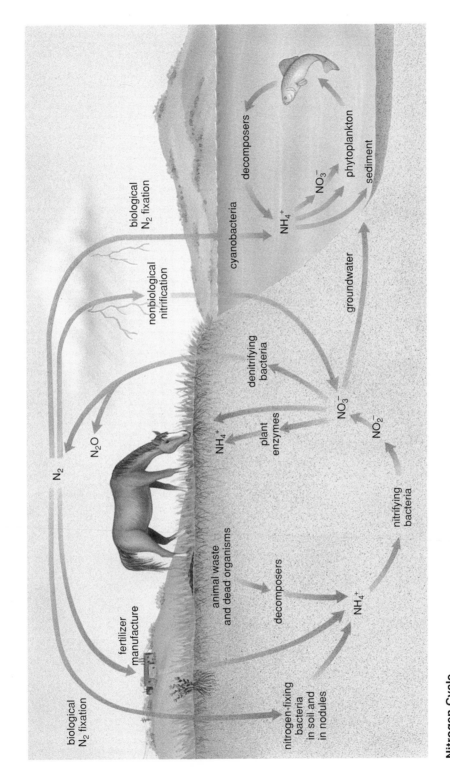

Nitrogen Cycle
Figure 50.10

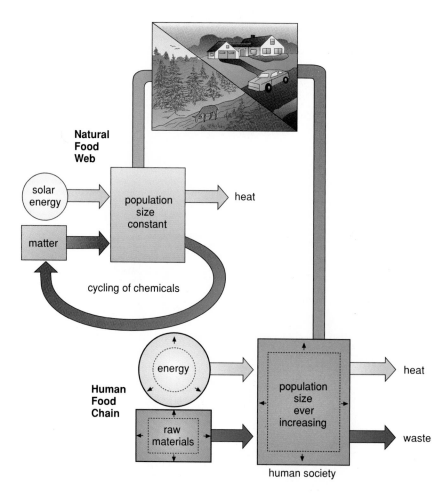

Natural Food Web vs. Human Food Chain
Figure 50.13

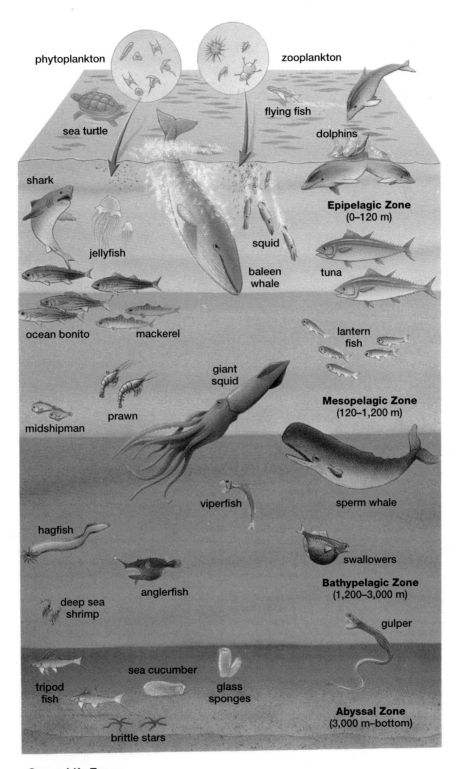

Ocean Life Zones
Figure 51.5

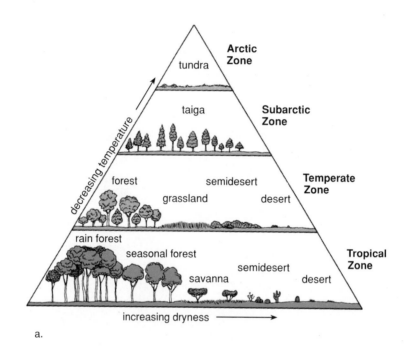

Temperature and Rainfall Determine Biome
Figure 51.6a

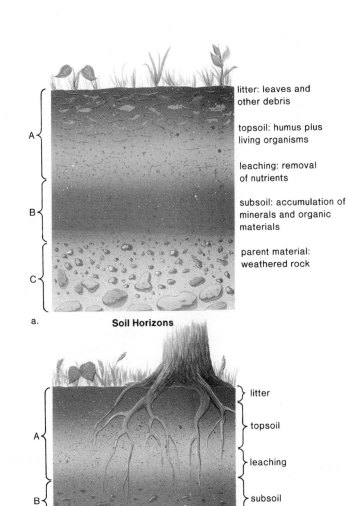

a. **Soil Horizons**

litter: leaves and other debris

topsoil: humus plus living organisms

leaching: removal of nutrients

subsoil: accumulation of minerals and organic materials

parent material: weathered rock

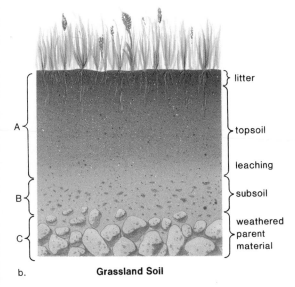

litter

topsoil

leaching

subsoil

weathered parent material

b. **Grassland Soil**

litter

topsoil

leaching

subsoil

weathered parent material

c. **Forest Soil**

Soil Profiles
Figure 51.9

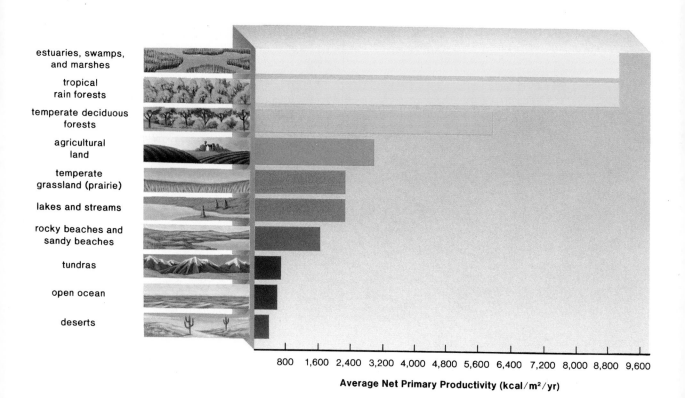

estuaries, swamps, and marshes

tropical rain forests

temperate deciduous forests

agricultural land

temperate grassland (prairie)

lakes and streams

rocky beaches and sandy beaches

tundras

open ocean

deserts

800 1,600 2,400 3,200 4,000 4,800 5,600 6,400 7,200 8,000 8,800 9,600

Average Net Primary Productivity (kcal/m²/yr)

Net Primary Productivity of Biomes
Figure 51.14

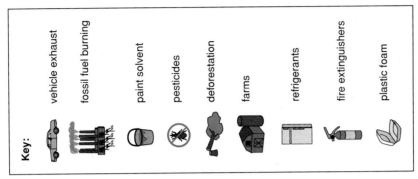

Key:
- vehicle exhaust
- fossil fuel burning
- paint solvent
- pesticides
- deforestation
- farms
- refrigerants
- fire extinguishers
- plastic foam

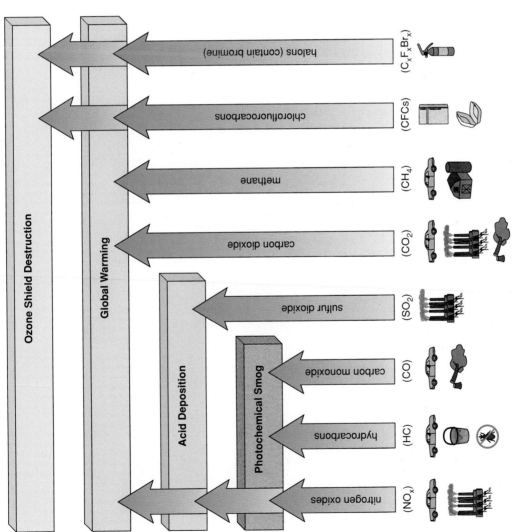

Air Pollutants
Figure 52.1

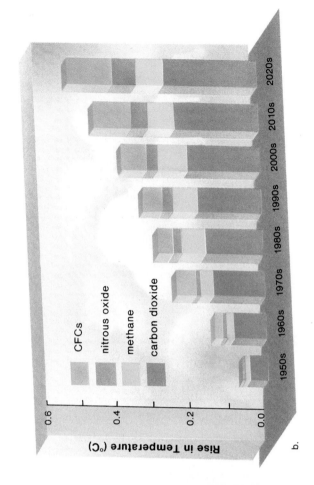

b.

a.

Global Warming
Figure 52.2

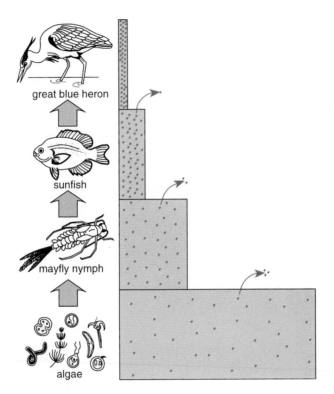

Biological Magnification
Figure 52.8

CREDITS

Line Art

Fig. 34.3b: From T. Elliot Weier, et al., *Botany,* 6th ed. Copyright © 1982 John Wiley & Sons, Inc., New York, NY. Reprinted by permission of the authors.

Fig. 34.8: From Kingsley R. Stern, *Introductory Plant Biology,* 6th ed. Copyright © 1994 Wm. C. Brown Communications, Inc. Reprinted by permission of Times Mirror Higher Education Group, Inc., Dubuque, Iowa. All Rights Reserved.

Fig. 34.9: From Kingsley R. Stern, *Introductory Plant Biology,* 6th ed. Copyright © 1994 Wm. C. Brown Communications, Inc. Reprinted by permission of Times Mirror Higher Education Group, Inc., Dubuque, Iowa. All Rights Reserved.

Fig. 35.7a: From Kent M. Van De Graaff, *Human Anatomy,* 3d ed. Copyright © 1992 Wm. C. Brown Communications, Inc. Reprinted by permission of Times Mirror Higher Education Group, Inc., Dubuque, Iowa. All Rights Reserved.

Fig. 39.8: From John W. Hole, Jr., *Human Anatomy and Physiology,* 5th ed. Copyright © 1990 Wm. C. Brown Communications, Inc. Reprinted by permission of Times Mirror Higher Education Group, Inc., Dubuque, Iowa. All Rights Reserved.

Fig. 40.5: From Kent M. Van De Graaff and Stuart Ira Fox, *Concepts of Human Anatomy and Physiology,* 4th ed. Copyright © 1995 Wm. C. Brown Communications, Inc. Reprinted by permission of Times Mirror Higher Education Group, Inc.,

Dubuque, Iowa. All Rights Reserved.

Fig. 43.6: From Kent M. Van De Graaff, *Human Anatomy,* 3d ed. Copyright © 1992 Wm. C. Brown Communications, Inc. Reprinted by permission of Times Mirror Higher Education Group, Inc., Dubuque, Iowa. All Rights Reserved.

Fig. 44.7: From Stuart Ira Fox, *Human Physiology,* 4th ed. Copyright © 1993 Wm. C. Brown Communications, Inc. Reprinted by permission from Times Mirror Higher Education Group, Inc., Dubuque, Iowa. All Rights Reserved. Reprinted by permission.

Fig. 45.5: From John W. Hole, Jr., *Human Anatomy and Physiology,* 6th ed. Copyright © 1993 Wm. C. Brown Communications, Inc. Reprinted by permission of Times Mirror Higher Education Group, Inc., Dubuque, Iowa. All Rights Reserved.

Photographs

Fig. 43.15: © From "Behold Man," Little Brown, and Co., Boston. Photo by Lennart Nilsson

Fig 45.2a: © Roger K. Burnard/BPS

Fig. 45.7b: © Biophoto Associates/Photo Researchers, Inc.

Fig. 45.10b: © Ed Reschke/Peter Arnold, Inc.

Fig. 50.1a-1: © Gallbridge/Visuals Unlimited